W9-BEK-765

# *Engaging Today's Students*

## WHAT ALL TEACHERS NEED TO KNOW *&* BE ABLE TO DO

### FOUR ESSENTIAL LEARNING COMPONENTS OF STUDENT ENGAGEMENT

Relevant Applied Learning

Student Choice

Student to Student Interaction

Assessment, Feedback, and Evidence of Success

By
Elaine M. Millen
Dr. Robert K. Greenleaf
Doris Wells-Papanek
Sharyn L. Orvis

*Greenleaf & Papanek* **Publications**

*Engaging Today's Students*
## WHAT ALL TEACHERS NEED TO KNOW *&* BE ABLE TO DO

**FOUR ESSENTIAL LEARNING COMPONENTS OF STUDENT ENGAGEMENT**
Relevant Applied Learning
Student Choice
Student to Student Interaction
Assessment, Feedback, and Evidence of Success

© *Copyright 2007 Greenleaf & Papanek* **Publications**
*First Edition*

*Greenleaf & Papanek* **Publications**

Contact Information

**Dr. Robert K. Greenleaf**
P.O. Box 186
Newfield, Maine  04056
207.793.8675 tel.
207.604.0089 cell

bob@greenleaflearning.com
www.greenleaflearning.com

**Doris Wells-Papanek**
1521 Heritage Court
Lake Forest, Illinois  60045
847.615.9957 tel.
847.615.9958 fax

doris@tailoredlearningtools.com
www.tailoredlearningtools.com

ISBN: 0-9767860-6-0  ~ Grades 5-12 Edition of Engaging Today's Students

# FORWARD

Teachers are now responsible for a new level of education for their students. To prepare them for the increasingly technological job market and global society, educators must help students develop their executive functions of prioritizing, reasoning, judgment, synthesis, and analysis. Students need guidance to *uncover* their higher cognitive, communicative, and collaborative skills as well as to *cover* the curricular material, and *discover* their roles as lifelong learners with capacities to apply the strategies and knowledge they learn as they are called upon to adapt to an ever-changing knowledge base and global challenges. Creative thinking outside the box is no longer an option. The lid is off the box and adaptability as well as critical thinking are as vital to learners as their in-depth proficiency with subject matter.

*Engaging Today's Students ~ What All Teachers Need to Know & Be Able to Do* is on-target and will resonate with all educators who recognize the changing demands that are being placed upon the students they teach. As a neuroscientist, I am particularly impressed by the level of understanding of the complex neurology of learning evident throughout the book and imparted to readers in clear, accurate, reader-friendly text.

Cogent suggestions are offered that will enhance instructors' effective building of their students' frontal lobe higher cognition through relevant learner-centered assignments, personally relevant choice and goals, neuro-*logically* paced class work, opportunities (for) real world application of understanding, differentiated instruction, intrinsically engaging and challenging class work, and authentic assessments that incorporate creative problem solving and ongoing, formative feedback.

Reading *Engaging Today's Students ~ What All Teachers Need to Know & Be Able to Do* takes you on a well-guided journey between the brain and the successful, interactive, and collaborative classroom, as you gain in-depth understanding of the innovative, brain-research based strategies that enrich the time students spend in your classroom. Specific examples, student responses, end of chapter questions to stimulate your own mental manipulation, well-constructed diagrams, and an appendix filled with programmatic applications of the strategies described, make this book practical as a reference to return to as you continue to build your effectiveness in the classroom. Emphasis is rightfully placed on how to engage students in self-motivated acquisition of knowledge, and engage them through experiences that enhance their proficiencies to perform targeted tasks, and to apply *what* they know as well as their expanded *way of thinking* to future occupations and lives.

Judy Willis, MD, M.Ed.

# DEDICATION

To Duffy,

Through your love and patience you have made me a better person. Through your support and encouragement you have made me a life long learner.

**Elaine Millen**

To all the "teachers" I've had the privilege to know throughout my educational journey, my professional life, and... most importantly... in my personal life. And to my two wonderful daughters, who have taught me so much about life, love, and the passion for learning.

**Sharyn L. Orvis**

# TABLE OF CONTENTS

## Purpose of the Book

In this book, we have examined the research around learners of today (grades 5-12), the brain sciences (with respect to learning), and effective teaching practices that link to long-term memory and recall. We have observed hundreds of classroom lessons and activities, developed by an array of practicing school teachers. A strong indicator for how we organized this book was our deep commitment to learners ~ students as learners AND faculty as learners ~ and how we all can learn in significant ways that are also sustainable.

## Organization of the Book

This book is organized so that the reader can begin to transform the instructional planning process to meet his or her needs in understanding the areas of relevant applied learning, student choice, student interaction, and feedback/assessment. For example, if applied learning were an absent component of a unit design, this text provides guidelines to support an instructional shift. Whether moving full speed ahead embracing the entire package or taking smaller incremental steps toward practices that engage the learners of today is at the discretion of the teacher.

Ultimately, this book has been developed with the intention of improving the quality of teaching and learning in the day-to-day classroom. To have an impact on student achievement outcomes, we must adjust the way we think about the system of educating students and make the changes that reflect the realities of today's society and the influence it has had on the needs of the students we encounter.

### Introduction

Chapter ONE, page 3

We are challenged to transform our classrooms so that we enable all learners to learn... *well*. We know that to meet this goal, teachers need to fully understand that today's learners want to make sense of their world, to find meaning in the educational environment, and support for their beliefs, values, and behaviors. Good instruction connects learning to what is known to be important *to the student*.

### Today's Students

Chapter TWO, page 5

At a time when critical thinking and problem solving is increasingly valued both for individuals and lifelong development, education has never before been more challenged with the question "How do I ensure that all students have the capacity to be successful in their lifelong academic and workforce endeavors?"

### Foundational Components

Chapter THREE, page 12

As societal demands have shifted, so have student dispositions and learning needs. The paradigm shift in education is moving from coverage of information to student learning that is organized around key outcomes.

## Overview of the Book by Chapter

### New Paradigm

Chapter FOUR, page 70

Implementing this engaging approach to teaching requires new curriculum and unit development processes for educators. The vision of the role of the teacher as the facilitator of learning requires creating a culture of continuous learning that is flexible, student-centered, and collaborative.

### Administrator's Role

Chapter FIVE, page 94

The administrator must take part in this process. S/he is essential to the support needed for teachers to convene, communicate ideas and concerns, and to experiment with facets of this framework. Their success will be exponentially greater if they work as partners. It is the leader's role to ensure that efforts are encouraged, practices implemented, and progress monitored.

### Conclusion

Chapter SIX, page 99

The challenge of transforming our classrooms is a priority in this changing educational climate. Policy and system leaders must recognize the need to examine present practices and support these new issues for a global economy. It is our belief that the teacher who interacts closest to the learner makes the most difference, one-step at a time.

## Chapter **ONE**

# INTRODUCTION

**SETTING THE STAGE**

Students in the 21ˢᵗ century are on a lifelong educational journey. Never before have we been confronted with so many questions about what is essential to learn, with such a short amount of time in which to learn it. Some students have embraced this challenge against all odds. Others in today's classroom lack a connection to the learning and have become disengaged.

We are challenged to transform our classrooms so that we enable all learners to learn… *well.* We know that to meet this goal, teachers need to fully understand that today's learners want to make sense of their world, and need to find meaning in the educational environment in order to support their beliefs, values, and behaviors. Ever mindful of a rigorous curriculum, today's instructional approaches must connect learning activities to what is known to be contextually relevant *to the student.*

It is our intent to provide a frame for transforming the traditional unit of study outline into one that reflects a commitment to student engagement through:

- Relevant Application of Learning
- Student Choice
- Student Interaction
- Ongoing, Embedded Assessment.

"Fortunately, brain research has confirmed that strategies benefiting learning with special challenges are suited for engaging and stimulating *all* learners."

Willis, 2007.

*"...today the world is becoming tougher, more competitive, less forgiving of wasted resources and squandered opportunities. In tomorrow's world a nation's wealth will derive from its capacity to educate, attract, and retain citizens who are able to work smarter and learn faster- making educational achievement ever more important both for individuals and for society..."*

Higher Education Commission Report, 2006.

## DEMANDS AND CHALLENGES AHEAD

Across the nation, new demands are being made on educational systems. It seems like everyone is weighing in on the landscape of our practices, our purpose, and our outcomes.

While success stories are abundant, the feedback we receive is not always flattering.

It is clear that the challenge is far greater than to educate only a fraction of the whole. We have come to recognize that the diverse learners in this society have unique perspectives, habits of mind, and widely varied experiences. These students are filling our classrooms in record numbers and are certainly providing us with a challenge to keep them there... as well as to educate them well! As much as we might welcome advances in technology and the potential for their impact on instruction in the classroom, the purpose of the teacher has remained the same ~ to facilitate the learning of all students.

The question is how? Are there fundamental requirements for this new age of learners that differ from those we've become familiar with?

# Chapter **TWO**

## TODAY'S STUDENTS ~ Who Are They?

*"For nearly a quarter-century, America has made aggressive efforts to improve schools. There has been some progress: standards [expectations] are higher, the curriculum richer, the evaluation of student performance more sophisticated. But, if we are to see substantial performance improvements from all students, we need better performance from their teachers."*

Arthur Levine, 10.31.06.

**PREFACE QUESTION**

At a time when critical thinking and problem solving is increasingly valued both for individuals and lifelong development, education has never before been more challenged with the question "How do I ensure that all students have the capacity to be successful in their post-secondary endeavors?"

**STATISTICS ON TODAY'S STUDENTS**

For nearly a decade, the K-12 education reform movement has challenged educators at all levels PK-16 to raise academic standards and monitor student outcomes. This is based on the belief that the purpose of schooling is to give learners the knowledge and skills essential to be successful in today's global society. The findings in the recent Higher Education Commission report of 2006 make it clear that the face of our institutions today has changed significantly.

Here are a few statistics present in classrooms today that impact not only those who choose education beyond high school, but also each person ~ regardless of where they exit formal learning opportunities. We will encounter these in increasing measure over the next few years:

- 40% of all college students take at least one remedial course at an estimated cost to the taxpayers of $1 billion annually

- Industry spends significant financial resources on remediation and re-training of post secondary learners

- 90% of the fastest growing jobs in the new information and service industry require not only a high school diploma, but post-secondary education as well

- The Department of Labor projects that by 2014 there will be close to four million new job openings combined in health care, education, computer, and mathematical sciences

- In the global competition, we have slipped to 16th in high school graduation rates

- There are an unacceptable number of students who fail to complete their education, while those that graduate don't always learn enough to be successful in their field of study.

Higher Education Commission Report, 2006.

*"Students in the 75 more successful ...schools reported... that they often experienced:*

- *apprenticeships, work based opportunities*

- *emphases on applied learning strategies*

- *help in seeing the importance of their studies to their future*

- *[a shared] responsibility for learning."*

Gene Bottoms, 2006.

The new demands of information technology, education, and health care ~ the jobs our students will be seeking upon graduation from schooling ~ all require higher order thinking skills, and demand a new level of proficiency in basic skills. Yet, the students sitting in our classrooms today come to us with skills and varied learning styles that demand a set of instructional practices that very few of us have been prepared to deliver. Understanding what it will take to meet the needs of the diverse learner has become an enigma in the classrooms of today. We are challenged by questions such as:

- What is unique about these learners and how do I guide them to reach their learning potentials?

- How can students be helped to see that their investment in learning TODAY is critical to their success tomorrow?

- How can I engage the students in their own learning?

- What "basic skills" for the knowledge economy are being addressed in my class(es)?

- How can I increase student accountability and improve learning outcomes?

"SCANS Workplace Competencies"

- Management of Resources: Time, Money, Materials, Facility, Human Resources

- Interpersonal Skills: Participates in Teams, Teaches Others, Leads, Serves Clients, Negotiates Decisions & Works with Diversity

- Acquisition, Organization, Evaluation and Use of Information

- Understands, Uses & Improves Systems

- Understands, Uses & Problem Solves Technology

- Basic Skills

SCANS Report, 2000.

*"As educators in rapidly transitioning schools, we need to reexamine everything we're doing. Continuing with business as usual will mean failure or mediocrity for too many of our students, as the data related to racial, cultural, linguistic, and economic achievement gaps demonstrate (National Center for Education Statistics, 2005). Rapidly changing demographics demand that we engage in a vigorous, ongoing, and systemic process of professional development to prepare all educators in the school to function effectively in a highly diverse environment."*

Gary R. Howard, 2007.

## WHO ARE TODAY'S STUDENTS?

If you have been involved in public education for a number of years, you have noticed a change in the makeup of your students that is adjunct with curriculum shifts, instructional requirements, an onslaught of strategies used to reach students, the types and numbers of assessments you do... and the procession of accompanying elements that follows. If you are fairly new to the profession, you may be thinking "Who are these kids, anyway? I wasn't this type of student!" Veteran or newcomer, the challenges facing public education today are mounting, and it is the student of this millennium that is at the core of our focus.

Why is this? The report of the *New* Commission on the Skills of the American Workforce, "Tough Choices or Tough Times," points out some global differences that have a large impact on both teaching and learning. This report points out, for example, that American students are, more than ever before, in direct competition with countries that:

- provide a better education to their students
- educate students to become highly informed workers willing to work for low wages
- digitize the work, requiring fewer workers
- access a worldwide workforce compiled of people who do not have to move to participate in truly global teams.

*"In a world in which knowledge is changing rapidly and technology is providing access to vast amounts of information, our challenge is not merely to give students more facts about geography, customs, or particular conflicts. Rather, our challenge is to hone students' critical-thinking skills and to familiarize students with key concepts that they can apply to new situations. In this way, they can make sense of the explosion of information from different sources around the world and put factual information into perspective and context. Only then can this information become meaningful."*

Vivien Stewart, 2007.

What does this mean for us, as teachers in public education? It's not about technology alone. We all know that technology provides us with significant instructional tools. What technology cannot provide our students, however, are the qualities that are most needed in the global competition for jobs and personal satisfaction:

- creativity and innovation
- facility with the use of ideas and abstractions
- the self-discipline and organization needed to manage one's work and drive it through to a successful conclusion
- ability to function well as a member of a team.

For us, that means we not only have to ensure that students reach proficiency in the basics, but we also must teach students how to think, to problem-solve, to be decision-makers, to use their imagination, to visualize, and to be creative. We need to teach them to be responsible, honest, collegial, and collaborative, and to have self-discipline. The jobs our students will be seeking upon graduation require all of these... and more. Yet, the students sitting before us, regardless of grade or demographics, bring with them an enormous diversity. Their skill levels range widely, their learning styles are varied, their backgrounds and ethnicity have a "culture" all their own.

*"For the most part, the American education system has succeeded in preparing generations of students for a place in American society. Where it did not the economy had a place for people who were willing to work hard even without the skills of formal schooling. The demands of today's society are different. We need graduates that can compete in the global economy. We need adults who can use the knowledge and skills they acquire in school to deal with the complex issues of their own communities and of the world."*

National Education Goals
Panel, 1993.

**BREADTH OF THE ISSUE**

Educators, business leaders, legislators, and others agree that the improvement of the American institution must start with accountability for student achievement that meets the need of the new set of skills for the future. Employers perennially report that many newly hired graduates are not prepared for work, lacking the critical thinking, writing, and problem solving skills needed in today's workplaces. In addition, business and government leaders continue to urge all workers to embrace the true meaning of lifelong learning. Schools throughout the country are encouraged to collaborate with community and business leaders to solve real problems together, connecting the best of research with application and practical experiences. Many recent studies and reports have concluded that unless applied learning is at the focus of educational performance, future American workers will be unable to use the new technologies that will create most of the world's jobs and economic growth in this century. We are already being challenged in industry with the availability of high paying jobs and the lack of individuals with the skills to fill those jobs. Consequently, American companies continue to go abroad in search of skilled workers to fill management positions here in the United States.

"We need to end the old argument about whether teaching is a profession like law and medicine, requiring substantial education before one enters practice, or a craft like journalism to be learned on the job. Teaching is a profession. It requires deep content knowledge, a familiarity with ways to teach that knowledge effectively, and an understanding of how young people learn and grow."

Arthur Levine, 10.31.06.

With the average high school completion rate at 70%, many entering college or the workforce are not prepared to meet the increasing demands of the rapidly changing, technology driven marketplace. Today's post-secondary opportunities require individuals to work as a member of a team, to understand multi-leveled problems, design and implement solutions, and evaluate results for improved outcomes. Our schools must embrace the responsibility to ensure that these skills are a part of "what students should know and be able to do" throughout their educational experience.

Finally, access, innovation, and engagement will lead to increased opportunities to be entrepreneurial in the way we design our future in education, from implementing new methods of teaching and content delivery to supporting the increased needs of lifelong learning after high school and in the workplace.

# Chapter **THREE**

# FOUNDATIONAL COMPONENTS TO SUPPORT FRAMEWORK & PROCESS

As both school and workplace demands have shifted, so have student learning needs. The following excerpt from the short story "Entertaining an Elephant" portrays an all too common circumstance in education today.

Taken from...

**"ENTERTAINING AN ELEPHANT:** A Novel About Learning and Letting Go."

William McBride, 1996.

"…I've been teaching for fifteen years now, and I've got it down. I've worked very hard to develop my teaching system."

"System sir?"

"That's right, my system."

Opening his briefcase, Reaf pulled out his old, tattered lesson-plan book and tossed it on the desk. It landed with a loud snap. Yellow chalk dust sprayed into the air.

"It's all in here," he said smugly. The little man looked at Reaf, confused.

"Just name a date," Reaf said, leaning back in his chair and folding his hands behind his head.

"A date sir?"

"Sure, any date during the school year. Just name one."

"September second."

"No, no. Not today. That's too easy. A date in the future. Take February seventh, for example. Now, watch this."

Mr. Reaf leaned forward and picked up the lesson-plan book. Thumbing through the light-green pages, he came to the page marked "February 7" at the top. He then turned the book around and tossed it back on the desk.

"There now, what do you see?" he asked, leaning forward.

*"When teachers remain passionate about what they teach, students will remain motivated and engaged. If teachers have taught the material dozens of times before and reached the point of boredom, they should punch up the lessons by bringing in connections to their own interests or current world events. Teachers' enthusiasm will shape the emotional climate and interest level of their students."*

Willis, Judy. "Brain-Friendly Strategies for the Inclusion Classroom," ASCD, 2007.

The janitor leaned over the desk and studied the book for a moment.

"It says 'diagramming indirect objects.'" He looked up at Reaf, obviously still confused.

"That's right. Indirect objects. Come hell or high water, on February seventh I'll be teaching how to diagram indirect objects. I told you I worked hard. It took me years and years to work out this system. But every year now, with only a few minor adjustments because of holidays and assemblies, I know exactly what I'll be teaching on each and every day. Pretty impressive, huh?" Reaf leaned back in his chair.

"It does make an impression, sir," the janitor replied. "How long have you used this system?"

"Gosh, let me think. You know, I guess I started it about seven years ago, when things really started getting bad."

"Bad, sir? How so?"

"Well, teaching, and schools for that matter, used to be a lot different. For one thing, most kids came to school wanting to learn. They did the homework you assigned, they came to class with pen and paper, they showed you respect. Hell, even those who didn't give a damn acted decently on the whole. Sure, you had an occasional troublemaker, but all you had to do is call a parent and things usually got straightened out."

Reaf leaned back in his chair and stared out the small window across the room. "Teaching was fun then. I used to try all kinds of new things with the kids. But as kids got rougher, more disrespectful, more screwed up, I found I needed to clamp down on them more and more. …Shoot, kids used to get excited about wearing school colors on game day.

…I realized I had to start looking after my own survival if I were going to stay in teaching. I had only ten years until retirement. I felt it was worth hanging on."

As societal demands have shifted, so have student dispositions and learning needs. The paradigm shift in education is moving from coverage of information to student learning that is organized around key outcomes.

The focus, then, is on what students need to know and be able to do, rather than just the review and recall of isolated, "flat" information. This emphasis presents significant challenges to educators. Never before have schools been asked to ensure that all students achieve the essential knowledge and competencies, and never before have we been faced with such challenging and diverse student populations.

This new form of teaching and learning requires that the learning process be focused on how students think and understand, as opposed to only getting the right answer. A shift away from "point in time" learning must be replaced by instruction that is more flexible. By allowing students to develop knowledge over time and applying this knowledge to solve real life problems, students will have a deeper understanding of the content. Demonstrating the application of proficiency becomes the goal.

To develop higher order thinking skills, new instructional methods must engage learners in constructing their own understanding by playing an active role in the learning process.

*"High Schools That Work academic core also score higher… if they have teachers who bring traditional academic courses to life using practical and real-world examples that can be borrowed from the workplace."*

Gene Bottoms, 2006.

*"Rigor can only take students so far. For many students, if they cannot see a reason for learning academic content, they either dropout mentally or leave school[ing] altogether. When students encounter classes that are meaningful and relate directly to their future... achievement rises."*

Gene Bottoms, 2006.

Students are encouraged to take an increased responsibility for their learning by engaging with others, and choosing the level of application by solving problems that are significant.

These students are given the opportunities to explore current issues and concepts in depth, and their understanding of the knowledge base is developed over time, through experience.

Learning is emphasized rather than completing assignments and activities, and this is done both in and outside of the classroom. Instruction and assessment are integrated.

## Historical Approaches

Education is organized around a sequence of subject matter. Curriculum is covered; instruction paced by the term schedule; assessment occurs at timely intervals and may be driven by selected text.

Learning is organized around required curriculum in subject matter areas; a diploma is awarded based on grades and the accumulation of credits

Curriculum is derived from existing content, usually determined by textbooks.

Assessment is done at standard intervals and more often than not focuses on skills that are assessed through paper and pencil responses. Grades are based on cumulative averaging.

## Emerging Approaches

Emphasis on high levels of learning for all students; pace of instruction is based on learning not coverage; differentiated instruction, learning styles, and diversity are all addressed through instruction, so that all students can learn.

Learning is organized around what students should know and be able to do; credentialing is based on student demonstration of proficiency of the knowledge and skills.

Curriculum is derived from learning outcomes and is based on what students should know and be able to do; content is integrated around real-world problems that require reasoning, problem solving, and communication.

Assessments reflect what students understand and can do; performance based assessments are used to assess student proficiencies, and grades are based on cumulative knowledge.

Achieving the transformation of education that we are talking about requires new roles and new skills for teachers. They are instrumental to the success of educational changes, through their willingness to be transparent and innovative about their work. This means that teachers will have to take risks, and to invest considerable professional development time to adapt and implement the revised learning outcomes. New methods of instruction and assessment will replace the comfort of delivering a curriculum that is based on input and routine quizzes or testing. In its place will be far more discrete exchanges of assessments and feedback in more compact segments.

## Student Learner Pedagogy

The constructivist theory of teaching and learning has aligned the principles of pedagogy more solidly with needed practices. The most pertinent constructivist principles of learning include the following:

## Principles of Today's Learners

Learning is contextual. People learn in relation to what they already know, and what they believe. They come to the learning situation with knowledge gained from many previous experiences, and that prior knowledge influences what new knowledge they will create from the new learning experiences.

Learning is active rather than passive. People need opportunities to apply new understandings, and to reconcile them with their previous ideas and experiences.

Each new meaning enables people to develop deeper understandings and critical insights into how they think and what they know.

It takes time to learn ~ application at all levels has the highest probability of sustained understanding over time.

## Instructional Practices Based on Today's Learners

Include students in defining the purpose of assignments, to ensure that they are relevant to them.

Nurture student's interests in specific areas that are tied to learning and achievement.

Take individual needs and learning styles into account. Discuss what type of practice and feedback would be most helpful.

Use learners past experiences in the learning process.

Frame the learning process as a problem-solving, authentic task, and engage the students in experiences that challenge their present way of thinking.

Encourage student inquiry by asking open-ended questions.

Create a climate that is challenging, but not threatening.

Encourage innovative thinking that may have an impact on the future.

## Learner(s) of Today...
## How Do We Instill Motivation?

MOTIVATION
AND TODAY'S
STUDENTS

How to generate motivation in *all* learners has become the million dollar question for educators ~ at all levels. Most researchers believe that motivation is a concept that explains why people think and behave the way they do. It is difficult to understand, and to measure. However, we do know that our cultural context and cultural practices significantly influence our motivation.

Sociologists and anthropologists acknowledge that learning is impacted by social context (relevant applied learning), negotiation on learning (student choice), collaboration (student to student talk), and feedback format and frequency (assessment). In general, learning will be sustained if we embrace the view that human beings have an intrinsic motivation, are curious and active, make meaning from experience, and desire to be effective at what they value.

Constructing teaching and learning strategies that embrace this culturally responsive teaching mindset will promote constructive learning dispositions. Deliberate, explicit instructor actions can enhance a student's motivation to learn. This strategy involves constructing a learning culture in which the learner desires the information/knowledge, has the opportunity to contribute a personal insight, and has the ability to apply the skill in an innovative and perhaps non-traditional way. For example, this teaching strategy is framed around:

*"I think the stuff we learn in school now has nothing to do with my future or my life outside of school. It's boring..."*

Student, 2007.

- An essential question (the strategy), which may lead to curiosity and personal relevance (motivation)... OR

- A relevant global challenge in the content (strategy), which may lead to interest and/or the need to contribute to the good of all people (motivation).

The context of the classroom can energize an individual's learning, and promote engagement of the learner in the process so that learning is more sustainable. The student engagement framework represented in this book combines the essential motivational conditions and the understandings of brain processing for sustained learning into an instructional model for teaching and learning in our classrooms.

**MOTIVATION GRID CONTINUUMS**

Following is a grid that may be useful in assessing real or perceived motivational elements in our curriculum. The vertical continuum of the matrix runs from the notion of student choice (elective) to teacher-directed (non-elective). This suggests that some assignments may have the flexibility for faculty to provide opportunities for learners to direct their work in areas of interest (personal or avocation), or that the assignment is structured such that the instructor wants students to follow the format as provided. The horizontal continuum of the matrix illustrates the level of intended or perceived value. How important is this assignment? How much importance does the learner place on it? Is the student able to discern how importance may be derived from it?

## Student/Learner Motivation Grid

The Motivation Grid provides an opportunity to view the type and range of activities/assignments planned for students.

INSTRUCTIONS for each assignment you request:

1. Rate the assignment on the vertical continuum (i.e. to what extent is this assignment guided by student choice/design (top) or by teacher design without student input (bottom ~ non-elective?) [1 = full student design/choice, 7 = full teacher design/choice]

2. Now rate the assignment on the horizontal continuum (i.e. to what extent is this assignment viewed as important *to the student*?) [1 = not viewed as important to the student, 7 = very important to the student and his/her world]

3. Plot the intersection of each pair of coordinates (first rating and second rating) on the grid

4. After plotting several assignments you will require in the unit of study, look to see where the majority reside. Consider these as they relate to your intentions for the unit, and their impact on student learning outcomes

5. Ask students to do the same exercise, plotting their perceptions of each assignment

6. Compare the students' plots with yours to determine differences. Consider reasons for any differences.

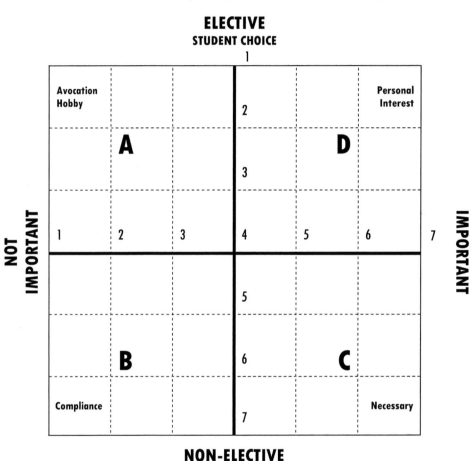

**THE FOUR GRID CORNERS**

Each corner of the Motivation Grid suggests an intersection of the continuums. For instance, the upper left corner merges high interest with little relative importance. This suggests an assignment that is of interest to the learner, but of little perceived usefulness in achieving key learning outcomes. The lower left corner intersects little perceived importance with required tasks, thus the role of the learner is one of compliance. The lower right corner is deemed necessary; the teacher requires it as part of the assignment, even if student interest is initially low. Finally, the upper right corner intersects both interest and importance. Clearly, if both of these elements are high, then learner motivation is heightened through personal interest and identified purpose.

"However teachers do it, making material authentically meaningful to each learner is crucial. If students can't relate to the new material, their neural networks will be less able to process it and retain it as memory, leading to frustration and discouraging classroom experiences."

Willis, Judy. "Brain-Friendly Strategies for the Inclusion Classroom," ASCD, 2007.

GRID
INTERPRETATION

**Motivation Grid: Interpretation of Plotting Results**

**Cardinal** Assignments located to the left of the vertical continuum need to move toward the right, if learning outcomes are to be maximized, both in the present and for long-range applications.

**Left/Right Placements** Assignments to the right of the vertical line could be a blend of what is necessary, and what is of personal interest (relevant/applied/personal meaning).

**Teacher/Student Differences** Any substantial difference between teacher perception and student perception should be discussed with students to determine where the discrepancy exists. Not all differences need to create changes in assignments. Careful consideration, however, is warranted to insure that the assignment(s) reside to the right side of the grid, even if students do not perceive them as such. The result could be a more defined purpose for the work that increases student understanding.

**Student Majority** If several of the students place an assignment anywhere to the left of the vertical continuum, then it must be assumed that the assignment's value is not clear to the learners ~ and as such, must be assessed for purpose and effectiveness.

**Top/Bottom Differences** If most assignments are placed below the horizontal line, it behooves the teacher to look into current student needs and interests toward adjusting assignments to be more applied (relevant to student needs/interests).

**Quadrant A** Assignments placed in this quadrant are generally unproductive toward key curricular goals. While they may be of interest to students, they remain essentially unnecessary toward important learning outcomes.

**Quadrant B** Any assignment that is perceived as unimportant work and is completed out of compliance only ~ will not result in useful, sustained learning. Revisit how the assignment functions for student learning needs.

**Quadrants C & D** When student interest, need, and unit of study outcomes are merged in assignments where learners can transfer the objectives or purpose of the learning to personal or work situations, sustained learning increases.

**MOTIVATION**
*&* **UNIT OF STUDY QUESTIONS**

**Questions Regarding Unit of Study Assignments**

1. Are the assignments clustered, or spread out?

2. Do the assignments contain the elements that help learners understand their importance, meaning, or purpose?

3. Have the students rated each assignment, both as it is given as well as after it has been accomplished?

4. How do the students' perceptions or understandings of the assignment(s) compare with yours?

5. Would any of the assignments benefit from alterations that would create more explicit understanding of purpose, relevance, and application?

6. If the learners perceive little importance, is there a way of constructing their understanding or adjusting the assignment to increase the level of importance or relevance perceived by the students?

7. If the students have interest, but feel the work has little importance to them, is there a way of making the work more explicit as to purpose?

8. If the learners are complying as a function of meeting requirements, is there a way to help them understand where or how this might be of interest or purpose ~ to increase learning outcomes?

Modified Student/Learner Motivation Grid
Source: Balance, Inc.., Creative Mind Systems, 1989.

Revisions by Robert Greenleaf, Greenleaf Learning, 2007.

## The Four Essential Components of Student Engagement

OVERVIEW Engaging today's students has become a major topic at State department of Education and individual school meetings, as well as at national professional development conferences. The complex relationship between motivation and the social culture of today's learner is now more important than ever to the instructional design and strategy. Educators need a model of teaching and learning that meets the needs of the unique learners in classrooms today and still maintains the rigor and high standards required to move into the post-secondary opportunities of tomorrow. The Student Engagement Framework provides this understanding.

This framework:

- Addresses the essential motivational conditions that are critical for learning to occur for the diverse learner

- Provides a structure for planning and applying an array of rich instructional strategies that will engage the learner in higher order thinking skills

- Is a holistic and systemic representation of four connecting, engaging constructs that instructors and students can create or enhance in their present practice

- Is respectful of the challenges in classrooms today, and can be used at the discretion of faculty in a way that has meaning for them, as well as the students.

The four essential components of student engagement are:

- Relevant Applied Learning

- Student Choice

- Student to Student Interaction

- Assessment, Feedback, and Evidence of Success.

**These are elaborated at length in the following pages.**

**27**

### Relevant Applied Learning

Essential ONE, page 29

New learning needs to be connected to previous experiences. Any theory and/or concept must have relevance for the learner, either through the connection to current events or the recognition that the learning experience has value.

### Student Choice

Essential TWO, page 41

Autonomy and self-direction is critical for the learning process. Instructors must serve as facilitators, rather than as directors of the learning.

## Overview of the Four Essential Components of Student Engagement

### Student to Student Interaction

Essential THREE, page 46

Social relationships are important to the learner, and have a direct impact on depth of knowledge. Connections to other disciplines and the extension of information are enhanced through social interactions that require both receptive and expressive language processing.

### Assessment, Feedback, & Evidence of Success

Essential FOUR, page 57

Clear outcomes are important to all students. Regardless of the grade, teachers must explain to students what they will "know and be able to do" as a result of being engaged in this learning experience. Then, intermittent feedback on key learnings is essential, for processing to long-term memory.

## Essential ONE

> *"I think students feel like they don't use much of their education in their current lives, because they don't do work that involves real-life situations very much, and they don't really know why they're learning what teachers are teaching."*
>
> Student, 2007.

## Relevant Applied Learning

At the forefront of this framework is the importance of personal relevance/applied learning and its relationship to engagement. Work and learning are particularly vulnerable to a powerful condition of disengagement. Unlike so many other behaviors in education, disengaged students threaten us not so much with something bad that will happen, but with the possibility that nothing may happen. When students are asked why they are disengaged from the learning process, they give the following responses:

- They feel constrained by the content and context of the knowledge (no empowerment)

- They see the knowledge, skills and attitudes as meaningless (information feels "flat" ~ for it's own sake)

- The curriculum lacks interest and challenge

- The work is repetitive.

In recent years, the research around the brain and learning has turned the paradigm on its side. The application of learning and of applying learning outcomes to solve real-world and personal challenges must be at the center of instructional planning, rather than as the culminating activity. It is the thread that holds the learning outcomes together.

> "…before we assign a challenge to our students, we ask, 'why would anyone really need to know this? What real-life roles might our students play if they were using this information?"
>
> Reeves, D. "Five Top Tips to Improve Student Engagement," Dec. 2006.

## LEARNING NEEDS OF TODAY

New learning needs to be connected to a life experience base. Any content or concept must have relevance for the learner, either through a connection to current events or the recognition that the learning experience has value.

The learning must be applied to students' lives or the world around them to have meaning and relevance. Authentic problems or challenges must be the foundation of the work in order to internalize the theory and concepts. From this, life is breathed into the content of the curriculum.

Relevant, applied learning is the domain for assessment and will take place within the context of the subject.

Problem solving is the center of applied learning. Using tools and techniques only becomes meaningful in the learning process when it is considered in the context of purposeful work. Applied learning is the capacity to use tools and techniques in an integrative way, in a real task. Context is critical to applied learning, and learning is practiced in context, not as an isolated skill.

Students are expected to demonstrate their knowledge in the context of problem solving projects or assignments. It is critical for students to clearly make the connection to the key outcomes of the unit under study. Applied learning produces a product or performance that can be used to provide concrete evidence of student achievement.

*"We learn absorbency and rubber band elasticity, for example, but not much that is useful for now or later. I mean, come on…it's not likely that I will grow up and work at a paper towel lab checking out the absorbency rates of Bounty or Viva."*

Student, 2007.

"[A] stressed state happens when a lesson is tedious, not relevant to their lives, confusing, or anxiety-provoking. In this state, the information doesn't pass through the amygdale to the higher thinking and memory centers of the brain."

Willis, Judy. "Research-Based Strategies to IGNITE Student Learning," ASCD, 2006.

**RESEARCH** &
**THE**
**FORMATION**
**OF MEMORY**

All long-term memory (LTM) is emotionally tagged. This means that meaning must be generated *by the learner,* or it has not been stored in the proverbial LTM "barn." Students must relate to the curriculum from their point of view. According to Judy Willis, "Relational memory takes place when students learn something that adds to what they have already mastered; they engage or expand on 'maps' already present in the brain."

Without meaning, value, or perceived usefulness, most material is taken from the instructor and given back on a test or in a written piece. This process relegates much to our short-term, working memory. If we are to develop *long-range* recall and understanding, we need to "attach" our new learning to something of value to us ~ something that has meaning. Otherwise, semantic memory ~ demanded most for rote learning, is fragile and soon forgotten.

"Rote memory is unfortunately the most commonly required memory task for students... This type of learning involved 'memorizing' and soon forgetting, facts that are often of little primary interest or emotional value to the student, such as a list of vocabulary words. ...With nothing to give [learners] context or relationship to each other or to the[ir] lives, these facts are stored in remoter areas of the brain. These isolated bits are more difficult to locate later because there are few nerve pathways leading to these remote storage systems." (Willis, 2006)

"Any new information must enter the brain through [the senses.] ...The information travels through [initial pathways] to the limbic system. After first entering the hippocampus messages are sent to the prefrontal lobe storage areas... to reactivate any potentially related memories stored there. ...previously stored, related memories can be activated and sent to [appropriate areas] where they are connected to the new information to build relational memories [requiring meaning in order to pass through]. The brain then makes the conscious connections between these stored memories and the new information, and forms a new integrated memory for storage in the frontal lobe."

Willis, 2006: p. 15.

**RESEARCH ON CONTEXT AVAILABILITY**

Before engaging learners in our curriculum, it is wise to reflect and consider that we, the instructors, have the intended body of knowledge or set of skills BEFORE instruction happens (please refer to the illustration on page 33: right side, bold circle). However, our students do not. This difference is crucial. We already know why some of the knowledge is key or pivotal, why certain skills are needed ~ as well as the big ideas that drive purpose and understanding. Students don't. Devoid of this context, forming meaning is hit or miss... difficult and unlikely.

Each concept, each lesson, and/or each big idea needs to be embedded in a context ~ a place for the mind to best "hold it," while it processes to establish meaning/purpose. Providing, or building a context in which the new material may reside while meaning can form, goes a long way to helping learner memory and recall. Thus, students can do more than just regurgitate curricular components back to us... they can process it sufficiently for long-term memory, recall, application, and transfer to the world beyond the classroom.

Contextual Learning occurs in close relationship with actual experiences. This type of learning allows students to test their ideas and theories against applications in their environment.

## Essential Unit Planning Components

The diagram below portrays a model that illustrates general schemata we can consider in using approaches that help learners build meaning. The intent is to help learners create a context for meaning to form ~ as early in the process as possible (perhaps even prior to exploring new, major ideas, chapters, materials, etc.).

The teacher understands the context for meaning (bolded circle on the right hand side) that applies to the class material to be covered.

The student does not.

Constructing a context helps the learner better understand how and why meaning or purpose is derived.

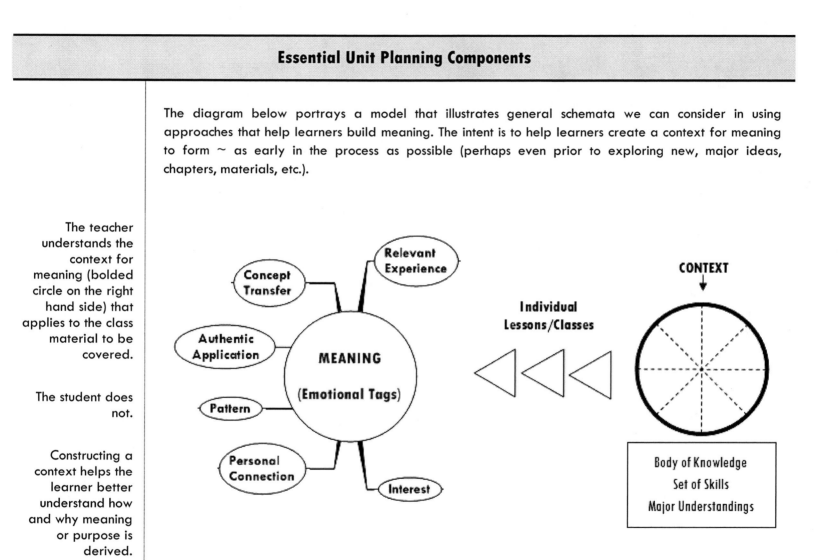

Constructing context via processing opportunities (such as those around the left circle as in the illustration on page 34) help the learner to understand how meaning may be constructed *for him/her*. The teacher understands the context for meaning (bolded circle on the right hand side) that surrounds the various components, lessons, or classes students will encounter in the unit of study. The student does not. It is simply NOT sufficient that the *instructor* understands the importance, application, or meaning of the curriculum. It is imperative that the *learner* gains this perspective, if s/he is to form long-term memory, recall, and effective transfer of learning to opportunities and new circumstances.

COMPONENTS
OF APPLIED
LEARNING

**Applied Learning**

1. Emphasizes problem-solving

2. Recognizes a variety of contexts for teaching/learning to take place

3. Teaches learners to monitor their own learning approaches

4. Anchors learning in diverse life-contexts

5. Encourages peer interaction

6. Employs authentic assessments.

National Conference of State Legislators, www.ncsl.org, 2006: p. 1.

**DAGGETT'S QUADRANTS / CONTINUUM APPLICATIONS MODEL**

Good students can recite knowledge back to us in a variety of assessment forms. Exceptional learning requires a more thorough understanding about how learning is put into play in actual life contexts.

As the circular continuum on the following page suggests, gaining knowledge without application appears shallow, lacks purpose, and defies retention for effective use and application over time. As knowledge (skill or understanding) is applied explicitly in any single discipline, and even better... transferred across multiple disciplines... learners develop a more integrated understanding of the knowledge. While many teachers may require learners to apply their learning to abstract or simulated examples, this falls short (in terms of brain and memory) of direct, explicit application to their work, their life circumstance, or known challenges. Understanding the usefulness, meaning, and contextual application of new ideas and knowledge so as to apply the learning to actual, relevant circumstances... known or random... across various areas enables learners to make maximum use of the important aspects of the curriculum.

"When information is embedded with personal relevance form prior experience, interests goals or real-world connections, the new data go beyond rote memory into long term memory."

Gardner, Poldrack et. al. in Willis, 2007.

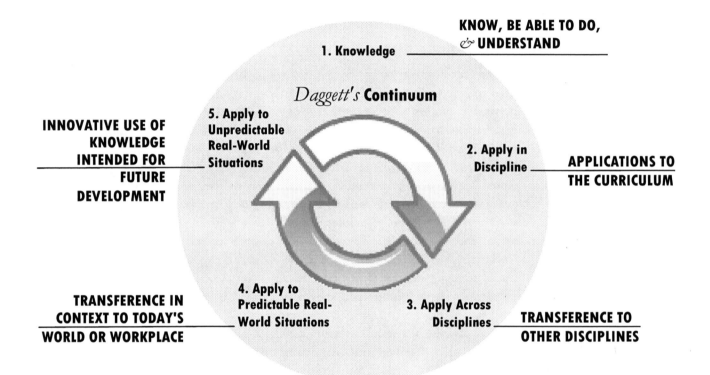

KNOW, BE ABLE TO DO,
*&* UNDERSTAND

1. Knowledge

*Daggett's* **Continuum**

INNOVATIVE USE OF
KNOWLEDGE
INTENDED FOR
FUTURE
DEVELOPMENT

5. Apply to
Unpredictable
Real-World
Situations

2. Apply in
Discipline

APPLICATIONS TO
THE CURRICULUM

4. Apply to
Predictable Real-
World Situations

3. Apply Across
Disciplines

TRANSFERENCE IN
CONTEXT TO TODAY'S
WORLD OR WORKPLACE

TRANSFERENCE TO
OTHER DISCIPLINES

**Terminology inside the gray circle: The International Center for Leadership in Education** www.daggett.com
The surrounding terminology is explained within the in the Comparison Table on the following page.

## Daggett ~ Engaging Today's Students Terminology Comparison Table

| Daggett Terminology | Engaging Today's Students Terminology | Explanation of ETS Terminology |
|---|---|---|
| 1. Knowledge | Know, Able to Do, *&* Understand | Identify key knowledge<br>Identify key skills<br>Clarify major understandings |
| 2. Apply in Discipline | Applications to the Curriculum | Build capacity to apply key knowledge, abilities and understandings to the discipline |
| 3. Apply Across Disciplines | Transference to Other Disciplines | Build capacity to apply key knowledge, abilities and understandings to the OTHER disciplines |
| 4. Apply to Predictable Real-World Situations | Transference in Context to Today's World or Workplace | Build capacity to transfer key learnings to real-world situations in the context of the learner's world and community |
| 5. Apply to Unpredictable Real-World Situations | Innovative Use of Knowledge intended for Future Development | Build capacity to use knowledge to transfer key learnings to real-world situations in the context of the learner's world and community AND apply to future needs and global situations |

**See pages 64-66 and Appendix G, beginning on page 117 for additional explanation and examples.**

## Questions to Ask about Relevant Applied Learning and its Use in the Unit of Study

It is vital for teachers to self-assess. Asking a few pertinent questions about the impact of the class as it relates to student applications in real contexts is important to the process of assuring relevant engagement.

**Questions for Teacher:**

- Have the current issues in the content of the unit of study been researched? Global challenges? Community problems?

- Do assignments and activities give students the opportunity to problem-solve the issues?

- Does the learner have the opportunity to apply the learning outcomes to meaningful personal issues?

- Are opportunities given to the learner to apply the knowledge, skills, and attitudes to current events within the content of study? Within other disciplines?

- Do students have the opportunity to relate key content to their social concerns and the broader concerns of society?

- Are learners encouraged to apply the learning in a non-traditional, "out of the box thinking" way?

## Questions for Students:

Feedback from students is also a source of important information for teachers. Obtaining student input is a tool to guide instructional decisions and to consider adjustments for assuring meaningful applications to the field and workplace.

- Has the content been researched with respect to current issues in your area? To global or local challenges?

- Do the assignments and activities give you the opportunity to problem-solve meaningful issues?

- Do you have the opportunity to apply important learning to meaningful personal issues?

- Are you provided opportunities to apply the knowledge, skills, and attitudes to current events within the content of your study? Within other disciplines?

- Do you have the opportunity to relate key content to the social concerns of your community and the broader concerns of society?

- Are you encouraged to apply the learning in a non-traditional, "out of the box thinking" way to new, innovative arenas of thought?

**KEY RESOURCES**
See Bibliography for Additional Information

Willis, Judy. *Research-Based Strategies to Ignite Student Learning.* ASCD, 2006.

Marzano, Pickering, and Pollock. *Classroom Instruction That Works.*

Reeves, D. "Five Top Tips to Improve Student Engagement,"

Essential **TWO**

BUILDING
ENGAGEMENT
THROUGH
STUDENT
CHOICE

## Student Choice

What does the research say about student choice?

When students have control of their educational experiences, their ability to learn and retain the material increases.

In this culture of diversity, with the importance of accepting and respecting unique differences, teachers must encourage all learners to understand their own construction of meaning. This requires responsiveness to each student's style of learning, and, more importantly, a need to provide options for students to give feedback on their learning. From this perspective the student's voice is critical, and is demonstrated through student choice. The instructional goal is to match the learning process, whether it's through materials, activities, assignments, or formal assessments, to the abilities and the experiences of the learners. Completing tasks and assignments for the sole purpose of meeting requirements has left some significant gaps in our current students' knowledge base.

Learners today need to see the reason for the learning activities before they will fully engage in the learning. Choice ensures that the content is applied to their personally relevant goals. Without student choice in the instructional plan, learners may inevitably come to the conclusion that "this was a waste of time."

Ideas for improved student engagement...

CHOICE:

"A recurring theme of the research on motivation is choice. This does not mean that students have the choice of *whether* to engage in the assigned work, but it does mean that effective teachers can provide choices of *how* students engage in the work."

Reeves, D. "Five Top Tips to Improve Student Engagement...," Dec. 2006.

Autonomy and self-direction is critical for the learning process. Teachers must serve as facilitators, rather than as directors of the learning. Student interest and personalized perspectives are instrumental to engaging the learner, and teachers need to be very clear about how the work they are asking the student to do will get the student where they want to go. Students need to gather their own knowledge rather than being supplied with facts.

Barbara Given points out that, "The simple act of decision making powerfully enables students to take charge of their learning. ...After developing preliminary knowledge about the topic they study ...in multiple ways. ...choices about what materials are used... empower students to make decisions about how they learn." (2002)

Renate and Geoffrey Caine support student choice stating, "Humans have a biological imperative to make decisions in the moment. All students make thousands of moment-to-moment decisions; ...Decision making capabilities are built in to the brain, and they are invoked when students ask genuine questions focused on what matters to them. Such decision making can naturally lead to the development of new knowledge." (2006)

*"Homework Menus create a series of choices for students that will provide opportunities for proficiency for all students…"*

*"Some teachers create this in several columns and students choose one or two problems from each…"*

Reeves, D. "Five Top Tips to Improve Student Engagement," Dec. 2006.

TEACHER GUIDE

## Questions to Ask about Student Choice and its Use in the Unit of Study

It is vital for teachers to self-assess. Asking a few pertinent questions about the impact of the class as it relates to student applications in real contexts is important to the process of assuring relevant engagement.

### Questions for Teacher:

- Do I have a realistic understanding of the learner's goals, perspectives, and expectations of what is being learned?

- Have I adapted the assignment options to reflect the learner's levels of experience and skill development?

- Does the learner have the option to share a personal perspective through different assignment options?

- Do the varieties of assignments the students may choose from reflect different learning styles?

- Do the assignments allow the student to create a deep understanding of the knowledge, so that personal connections are possible?

## Questions for Students:

Feedback from students is also a source of important information for teachers. Obtaining student input is a tool to guide instructional decisions and to consider adjustments that assure meaningful applications to the field and workplace.

- Does the teacher have a realistic understanding of your goals, perspectives, and expectations for applying key learning outcomes?

- Has the teacher adapted the assignment options to reflect your levels of experience and skill development?

- Has the teacher provided the option for you to share a personal perspective through varied assignment options?

- Do the assignments vary to meet different learning styles?

- Do the assignments allow you to create a deep understanding of the knowledge, so that personal connections are possible?

**KEY RESOURCES**
See
Bibliography
for Additional
Information

Donegan, Billie, Greenleaf, Robert K., and Wells-Papanek, Doris. *Coaching Reluctant Learners.*

Teaff, Grant. *"Coaching in the Classroom: Teaching Self-Motivation,"* Cord Communications, 1994.

Greenleaf, Robert K. *Creating and Changing Mindsets: Movies of the Mind.*

Mitra, Dana L. *'The Significance of Students: Can Increasing 'Student Voice' in Schools Lead to Gains in Youth Development?'*

**See Appendix G, beginning on page 117 for additional Student Choice information.**

## Essential **THREE**

*"Sometimes students lack prior knowledge that might make obvious the significance of meaning… [This] reduces [student activity to that of the] rote learning of arbitrary associations, a process known to be difficult."*

Woloshyn, et. al., 1990.

## Student to Student Interaction

OVERVIEW

Both research and experience tell us how important it is for learners to be "engaged" in the work of learning. When students are highly involved in the work, then sustained, meaningful work takes place, resulting in application and transfer. One way to increase the probability of engagement is through interaction. Not just interaction as a class through question-answer or discussion, but through student-to-student interaction, or activity. This can take the form of small teams or even simple pairings. The options here are many, ranging from short term (1") to long term (weeks), and from quick exchanges of pairs to coordinated projects over time. Marzano, Pickering and Pollock's (2001) work places such cooperative ventures between learners as one of the top ways educational research supports noted increases in achievement outcomes (See Appendix D, page 113).

The importance of social relationships suggests that such interactions have a direct impact on the ultimate depth of knowledge gained. Recent work articulates that connections to other disciplines and extensions of information are generated through the social interactions between learners.

"When neurotransmitters are depleted by too much information traveling through a nerve circuit without a break [lecturing], the speed of transmission along the nerve slows down to a less efficient level. When this happens, information processing takes longer, leading not only to student frustration, but also to less successful memory storage."

Willis, Judy. "Research-Based Strategies to IGNITE Student Learning," ASCD, 2006.

*"In my classes, there are too many lectures and not enough hands-on activities. And I never get to talk to my friends, which is important to me."*

Student, 2007.

**SOCIAL CONSTRUCT**

The social interaction of students creates an environment of inclusion. Ideally, learners realize that different perspectives are part of their learning experience. Student to student interaction develops an attribute of connectedness that creates a climate inviting students to connect their experiences and histories with the new learning, reflect on others viewpoints, and communicate ~ all of which enhance the motivation to learn.

Using the social construct of the classroom as a teaching and learning tool embraces the basic principle that there is never a single transmitter of knowledge. In fact, we are collaborators in the learning process and this interactive strategy significantly promotes greater individual processing for memory.

This social construct of learning creates a setting in which learners:

- Validate their own learning through peer support
- Foster positive interdependence- understanding the value of unique contributions to solve problems and challenges
- Acquire new attitudes
- Receive social support and encouragement to take risks
- Respect and support the need for individual accountability
- Develop a better understanding of diverse cultures
- Recognize opposing beliefs and their impact upon the world
- Expand perceptions and perspectives on new knowledge. (Millen, 2006)

"A school must be a community of learners… with rituals designed to embrace each student into group membership; it cannot be just a place where students are obligated to spend time."

Given, 2002.

[There is] "… a relationship between the method of instruction and student on-task engagement."

Kumar, David, 1991: p. 50.

"Our personal identity is derived from the way in which we are perceived and treated by other members of our groups. We learn, work, worship, and play in groups. As humans we have an inherent social nature."

Given, 2002.

When learners interact with each other and speak, different neural pathways than those being used in listening are involved. Even brief exchanges can create electrical-chemical activities in the brain that serve to strengthen existing connections, and to generate additional pathways that serve to build a network of knowledge that is more contextually created and retrieved (receptive vs. expressive language).

Interaction between learners also creates opportunities for intermittent, reflective thought and processing. When students revisit their ideas and understandings throughout the learning process, their capacity to transfer recall is strengthened. It is *their* brain that is doing the work of recall, organizing, and forming knowledge, so to articulate. The only way to embed understanding for memory is to do the work *in one's own mind.* Requiring frequent interaction, even for very brief moments, can be enormously beneficial in the creation of improved memory and recall.

As stated by Woloshyn et. al., "Attempting to generate a response probably activates a network of information related to to-be-learned facts, even when learners cannot retrieve or construct information so that adequate answers to 'why' questions are produced." [Thus, learning for memory is enhanced by this action] (1990)

"The elaborative-interrogation effect [student generated] seems consistent with other demonstrations that learning is better when study includes active generation of information [conscious and effortful memory processes vs. being provided information]."

Woloshyn, et. al., 1990.

**RESEARCH THAT SUPPORTS INTERACTION**

Instructors have far too much to do, without creating more work for themselves ~ especially undertakings that result in little or no sustained learning outcomes. We work hard to be prepared, and sometimes fall into the trap of believing that we must know all, or have examples for everything. Student learning does benefit from examples, but not necessarily just those provided by the instructor. If we believe that s/he who *does* the work ~ learns, then we must engage students to do the work of generating the examples (when viable background knowledge and experiences exist).

Judy Willis writes: "If [students] draw a sketch of their visualizations and verbally communicate them to partners, or write about them in their own words, multiple brain pathways will be stimulated to enter long-term memory because they have personalized and interacted with the information." 2006.

The crux of memory is simple... the only person who can put new learning into the "barn" is the learner. No matter how hard we have worked as the instructor, no matter how extensive our expertise, we cannot *give* it to them for placement in long-term memory. Each learner needs to do the work (internal processing) necessary for memory formation.

"The goal of research-based education is to structure [learning] lessons to ultimately rely less on inefficient and tedious rote memory. Helping students access and use more effective types of memory storage and retrieval will literally change their brains."

Willis, Judy. "Research-Based Strategies to IGNITE Student Learning," ASCD, 2006: p. 6.

*In an exhaustive meta-study of education research over 35 years, Marzano, Pickering and Pollock identified NINE of the most effective strategies known to produce student achievement.*

*One of these was termed "nonlinguistic representations." Their review of the literature resulted in a finding that the use of nonlinguistic representations in the instructional forum produces an average gain of 26% over those not employing such.*

Marzano et. al., 2001.

## BI-MODAL MEMORY PACKETS

Left on our own, we all create and access imagery in our minds. For example, consider the thought of a certain parent, student, or neighbor heading your way. The first conscious activity in our mind is that of "seeing" an image of that person. The next conscious activity is the accompanying disposition or dominant emotion surrounding your relationship/experiences with that person. This is what our brain does automatically ~ naturally ~ as it processes and recalls ~ bringing prior experiences to consciousness.

Nonlinguistic, non-verbal representations can take many forms. They can be generated by instructor or learner in external fashion (graphic organizers, drawings, pictures, movement,) or from within the learner (prior experience and knowledge, imagery, imagination, sensory, reflections). Exposing the learner to representations that are provided by a publisher or by the instructor helps to create bi-modal packets (visual-verbal linked elements). When students either create their own representations in a medium or generate visuals in their minds, similar or even stronger memory benefits occur (Greenleaf & Wells-Papanek, 2005). Additionally, it makes little sense to focus on the process of creating memory if we don't give equal voice to the act of cueing memory, for recall and use at later times.

It is clear to the authors that, when the time comes to engage learners, bi-modal approaches are one vital way to accomplish greater student processing for initial memory, sustained memory, and recall.

Dual coding theory provides a model for understanding how the brain codes information (Paivio, Sadoski, Rieber, Tzeng, Tribble, Chu). "Memory packets" have two modes; linguistic and nonlinguistic. In essence, our system for storing information for later use and application is comprised of both verbal and visual elements. Bi-modal packets are just that ~ "bi"-modal. They have two separate but complimentary facets that, in combination, provide a greater capacity for constructing stronger, more durable, accessible memory.

Greenleaf & Wells-Papanek, 2005.

## Conducive Environments for Learning ~ Triangle of Personalization

Even with young adults (actually, all adults!), learning environments must be monitored regarding affective levels. Too much anxiety produces chemicals in the brain that make processing for memory far more difficult. Too little stimulation for meaning produces a state in which the attentional system may function for participation, but insufficiently for creating memory. A balance is needed.

The drawing below illustrates three vital aspects of creating an environment that supports maximal learning outcomes.

"The common theme to the brain research about stress and knowledge acquisition is that superior learning takes place when stress is lowered and learning experiences are relevant to students' lives, interests, and experiences."

Willis, Judy. "Research-Based Strategies to IGNITE Student Learning," ASCD, 2006.

## The Triangle of Learning Success or Inhibition

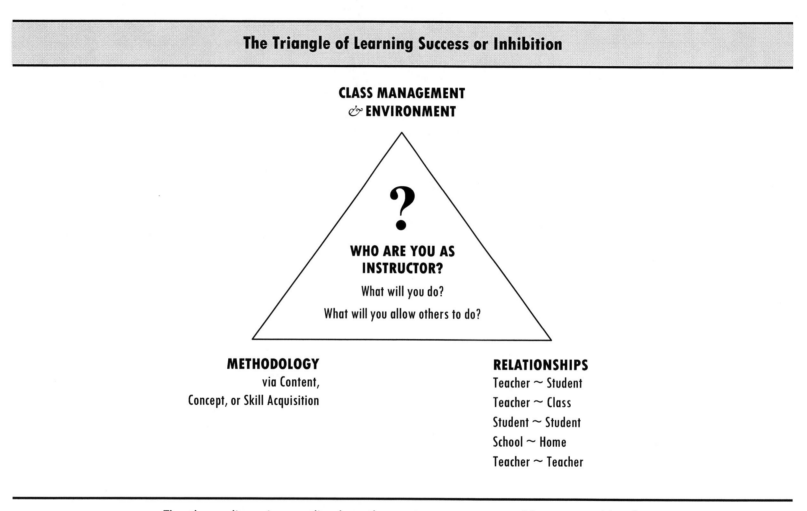

**CLASS MANAGEMENT**
*&* **ENVIRONMENT**

**?**

**WHO ARE YOU AS INSTRUCTOR?**

What will you do?

What will you allow others to do?

**METHODOLOGY**
via Content,
Concept, or Skill Acquisition

**RELATIONSHIPS**
Teacher ~ Student
Teacher ~ Class
Student ~ Student
School ~ Home
Teacher ~ Teacher

The three dimensions outlined on the next two pages provide opportunities for teachers to reflect on the overall environment in which students are being invited to learn.

CLASSROOM
MANAGEMENT

## LEARNING ENVIRONMENT

What interactions are common or prevalent in the classroom? What is their impact on others? Are students encouraged to participate? Do they freely participate? What percentage of the time? How do students treat/interact with other students?

| **Promotes Learning Success** | **Inhibits Learning Success** |
|---|---|
| Interactions are fostered | Interactions are primarily with the teacher |
| Interactions are constructive | Interactions are sometimes negative or destructive |
| | Interactions are scripted and directed by the teacher |

METHODOLOGY

## TEACHING *&* LEARNING APPROACHES

What strategies might best engage students for sustained outcomes? What approaches to the content and key learning targets would be best to help students learn the material or ideas?

| **Inhibits Learning Success** | **Promotes Learning Success** |
|---|---|
| Interactions are limited during class time | Interactions are frequently part of the class |
| Interactions are primarily with the teacher | Interactions are teacher constructed |
| Interactions between students are formalized and orchestrated | Interactions are student generated |
| Interactions are primarily as a whole class | Interactions are as pairs and small groups |
| Content is limited to text/info provided by the teacher | Content extends to personal experience/work |

RELATIONSHIPS

## ROLES *&* INTERACTIONS

What relationships are vital to form an environment where learning best happens? What needs to be considered for all students? What provisions may apply to any given individual student? Are there other, outside, extenuating circumstances that need attention? How will participants interact or treat one another in this class or unit of study?

| **Inhibits Learning Success** | **Promotes Learning Success** |
|---|---|
| Interactions are dominated by a few | Interactions involve all students |
| Interactions are primarily between teacher and student | Interactions occur between all parties |
| Interactions are limited to the curriculum being studied | Interactions extend to topics beyond the curriculum |
| Interactions typically involve the same student groupings | Interactions involve persons or things beyond the classroom (guests, on-site, etc) |
| Interactions are limited to those present | |

*"The best way to combine academic learning and natural learning is to create environments in which each student can pursue relevant questions while keeping curriculum goals in sight."*

Caine, Renate N. & Caine, Geoffrey. *"The Way We Learn,"* Educational Leadership, Vol. 64. no. 1. Sept. 2006: p.50.

TEACHER GUIDE

## Questions to Ask about Interaction and its Use in the Unit of Study

It is vital for teachers to self-assess. Asking a few pertinent questions about the impact of the class as it relates to student applications in real contexts is important to the process of assuring relevant engagement.

### Questions for Teacher:

1. Are students interacting with other students at least once each hour?

2. Are students interacting with different students from time to time?

3. Are students working in pairs for brief moments?

4. Are students working as teams for any purposes?

**Questions for Students:**

Feedback from students is also a source of important information for teachers. Obtaining student input is a tool to guide instructional decisions and to considering adjustments for assuring meaningful applications for meaning and with the outside world.

1. Are you interacting with other students frequently (every class)?

2. Are you interacting with several different students?

3. Are you interacting for brief moments as well as over time?

4. **Are you learning from your:**

|  | A LITTLE |  |  |  | A LOT |  |
|---|---|---|---|---|---|---|
| a. Materials or Readings? | 0 | 1 | 2 | 3 | 4 | 5 |
| b. Instructor's Methods? | 0 | 1 | 2 | 3 | 4 | 5 |
| c. Classmates? | 0 | 1 | 2 | 3 | 4 | 5 |

**KEY RESOURCES**
**See**
**Bibliography**
**for Additional**
**Information**

Greenleaf, Robert K. *Brain Based Teaching: Pairs Methods.* www.greenleaflearning.com.

Johnson & Johnson. *Cooperative Learning Methods.* www.co-operation.org/pages/cl-methods.html.

Kagan. Cooperative Learning Methods. www.kaganonline.com.

**See Appendix C, beginning on page 107 and Appendix D, page 113 for additional Student to Student Interaction information.**

## Essential **FOUR**

*"I think kids want to do well in school because that is what is expected by parents, teachers and others. They don't always give good effort, however, because these… years don't count toward… things in the future."*

Student, 2007.

*"Student assessment and program evaluation data need to be used to improve continuously the school climate, organization, management, curricula and instruction to advance student learning."*

Gene Bottoms, 2001.

## Assessment, Feedback, *&* Evidence of Success

OVERVIEW

Assessment ~ evidence of success ~ provides clear feedback for the learner, for reflection. When beginning a unit of study instructors must show students what they will "know and be able to do" as a result of being engaged in this learning experience. This needs to be clearly articulated at the beginning, so that all students understand what is expected. This is more than a chapter or unit guide. It is a concise accounting of key knowledge, skills, and understandings required of this segment of study. Accordingly then, assessment activities during each class, along the way, and at the conclusion of the unit or chapter must be aligned with the articulated expectations.

Assessment is not merely testing or the giving of a quiz here or there. Assessment opportunities range from the first moment of class to well after the unit has been completed. More importantly, the reasons for assessment eclipse the traditional scoring or grading purposes. For sure, we are deeply rooted in systems that require and issue ranks of one sort or another. However, assessment's greatest value (for learning) is in the feedback it provides to both the learner *and* to the teacher. This feedback is best acquired along the way, rather than after the chapter, unit or segment of instruction has been completed. Expanded ideas follow.

"Historically, a major role of assessment has been to detect and highlight differences in student learning in order to rank students according to their achievement. Such assessment experiences have produced winners and losers. Some students succeed early and build on winning streaks to learn more as they grow; others fail early and often, falling farther and farther behind.

Teachers and students are partners in the assessment for learning process.

Thus far, however, the immense potential of assessment for learning has gone largely untapped because we have failed to deliver the proper tools into the hands of teachers and school leaders."

Rick Stiggins, 2007.

**TEACHER FEEDBACK ALONG THE WAY**

The teacher provides students with formative feedback about key knowledge, skills, or understandings that underpin applications, meaning, and purposefulness of essential outcomes. This can be in the form of a quiz or other graded measure ~ but is most useful if conducted in a simple formative sense. Formative measures provide feedback that is useful regarding important learning outcomes ~ and are not graded. These measures simply "check in" with students to see how they are doing with the intended goals and outcomes of the unit of study. They allow students to adjust for improved learning outcomes and also provide information for the teacher to make adjustments as necessary.

**STUDENT FEEDBACK ALONG THE WAY**

Students provide each other or the teacher with formative feedback about their level of understanding "in progress," so that adjustments can be made by the student or by the teacher to ensure improved outcomes. Not all assessment feedback must be reviewed by the teacher. In many circumstances, students can provide each other with useful input toward better outcomes.

**PERCEPTIONS**

It is not just the curriculum, but the learner's disposition toward or about the curriculum that can provide insights as to motivation and performance that can be useful... at the onset of the unit of study, as well as during or after the classes have ended. A student who is off-track, and can be assisted to regain perspective along the way, will produce far better than one who is left to his/her own.

*"How much of this stuff am I able to use in my current life? None."*

Student, 2007.

"Because of the increased external stressors in today's society, it is crucial that we build supportive classroom communities in which our students retain (or regain) the excitement they felt when they entered kindergarten. Now more than ever, we need to make our classrooms safe, magical realms of fun, friends, discovery, and learning."

Willis, Judy. "Brain-Friendly Strategies for the Inclusion Classroom," ASCD, 2007.

**KNOWLEDGE, SKILLS, *&* UNDERSTANDINGS**

To wait until the end of a unit, chapter, or for weeks ~ to determine if a learner is "on target" or "off course," creates at least three learning issues:

1. The learner has been lost for too long a time, resulting in motivational or other troublesome issues

2. Inappropriate learning may have been reinforced, and must now be overcome

3. The entire responsibility for learning has been placed upon the student, with no expectation of teacher adjustments due to individual or class learning needs, and resultant performance along the way.

Getting and providing feedback frequently about the power standards (key learning outcomes) associated with each step or class along the way can serve to build understanding, long-term memory, and recall. If increased outcomes are desired, then intermitted assessment strategies must be employed.

**RESEARCH THAT SUPPORTS ASSESSMENT ~ BRAIN**

While the brain is being exposed to new material, we need to remember that exposure, even multiple repetitions of information, is not sufficient in most cases for memory strength (long-term) to form. There are a few "rules" for the overall development of memory, if assessment practices are employed to support long-term memory and recall, and not just short-term memory regurgitation.

> "…classroom assessment, like most things in education, enhances student achievement under certain conditions only:
>
> - Classroom assessment should be formative in nature
> - Formative classroom assessments should be frequent
> - Formative classroom assessments should give students a clear picture of their progress on learning goals and how they might improve…"
>
> ASCD Associate News, 2007.

## Lesson Review Patterns for Long-Term Memory
al la Schenck

RESEARCH
THAT
SUPPORTS
ASSESSMENT
~ BRAIN

In the first continuum, a common sequence of chapters, units, or segments of learning is illustrated. Units are taught, assessed, and then the next unit begins. A unit or chapter test typically follows each unit, and sometimes a "mid-term" or "final" follows several units of instruction ~ which spans back over several months of material. In this scenario, learners may do well on any given unit's assessment (designated by "A" after each unit sequence). However, students not only tend to cram the night before each unit assessment, they necessarily cram before a multi-unit, or final assessment, as the material has not been covered or reviewed for a long time. Even if cramming produces an acceptable outcome, long-term memory is less likely to be developed by this sequence of exposure to information.

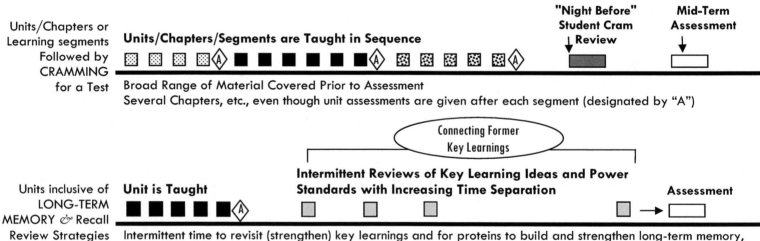

Units/Chapters or Learning segments Followed by CRAMMING for a Test

**"Night Before" Student Cram Review**

**Mid-Term Assessment**

**Units/Chapters/Segments are Taught in Sequence**

Broad Range of Material Covered Prior to Assessment
Several Chapters, etc., even though unit assessments are given after each segment (designated by "A")

Connecting Former Key Learnings

**Intermittent Reviews of Key Learning Ideas and Power Standards with Increasing Time Separation**

Units inclusive of LONG-TERM MEMORY *&* Recall Review Strategies

**Unit is Taught**

**Assessment**

Intermittent time to revisit (strengthen) key learnings and for proteins to build and strengthen long-term memory, and recall. Learning is cumulative, thus benefits accrue from past activities.

*"The most powerful single modification that enhances achievement is feedback. The simplest prescription for improving education must be "dollops of feedback."*

Hattie, 1992.

In the second continuum, where long-term memory is nurtured, the instructor reinforces important concepts and information through intermittent, increasing time separations (after the initial learning), to help students process additionally and more thoroughly ~ building the necessary chemical formations for stronger synaptic connections and thus, better recall. This can take place as a simple reminder, or as a quick, two-minute exercise. It can also be accomplished by a request to use the prior learning with the new material or in the upcoming project, chapter, or exercise.

Feedback... simple *informal* feedback... may be the most underutilized form of assessment FOR (rather than OF) learning readily accessible. Waiting until the teaching is over and then testing to see how learners have done on the material is TOO LATE! Providing and getting feedback along the way (at least weekly, if not daily) is essential to creating learning that lasts and is transferred into use. Otherwise, we are resigned to a primary focus of grading, in place of learning and achievement.

"Sivasailam Thiagarajan (Thiagi), ...stated that [people] only learn when they reflect on experience. ...reflective learning is the most powerful learning system, because it takes into consideration emotions, interactions, thoughts, and behaviors generated by the other learning systems. Reflective learning involves:

mentally recreating...

analyzing choices...

intellectually experimenting with strategies...

meta-cognitively monitoring and cultivating one's own thinking...

...constructing knowledge..."

Given, 2002.

*"...assessments designed for ranking are generally not good instruments for helping teachers improve their instruction or modify their approach to individual students."*
*They are:*

- *Taken too late with respect to the time of learning*
- *Feedback lacks detail needed to target specific improvements.*

**Robert Marzano, 2002.**

**Some quick bullets from studies regarding feedback include:**

- Feedback must be timely ~ immediate, or day after

- Feedback needs to be specific to a criteria, informing students where they stand relative to a specific knowledge or skill component

- Feedback can be provided by students, themselves, and/or by classmates

- Rubrics can be especially useful for providing more feedback than a single number or score

- Effective feedback explains what is accurate, and what is inaccurate.

"Consider what happens in music classes every day. When a student plays a note incorrectly, the music teacher does not record the error in the grade book and inform the student's parents nine weeks later that the student really needs to work on F-sharp. Music teachers continually assess student performance, stop when necessary to give specific feedback, and then immediately use that feedback to improve student's work.

The key to effective short-term wins is that the objectives are meaningful, are attainable, and provide immediate feedback to reinforce effective practice and modify ineffective practice. Without short-term wins, the pain of change often overwhelms the anticipated long-term benefits."

**Douglas Reeves, 2007.**

*Educators must Focus, Focus, Focus.*

- *"Which data, well analyzed, can help us improve teaching and learning?*

- *Within an identified subject/course, where do we need to direct our attention?*

- *Where do the greatest number of students struggle or fail within the larger domains?"*

Mike Schmoker, 2003.

**Teachers should ask themselves the following:**

- "Do my classroom assessments measure genuinely worthwhile skills and essential knowledge?

- Will I be able to promote my students' mastery of what's measured in my classroom assessments?

- Do my classroom assessments yield results that allow me to tell which parts of my instruction were effective or ineffective?

- Do my classroom tests take too much time away from my instruction?" (W. James Popham, 2003).

Three stages to the backward design process:

- "First: Determine student-learning goals

- Second: Collect, analyze and interpret evidence from multiple sources of data to determine how students are doing

- Third: Consider the root causes of present achievement levels and then ~ and only then ~ implement systematic actions to address root causes, promote enduring learning, and increase test scores."

Jay McTighe and Ronald S. Thomas, 2003.

## DIFFERENTIATED ASSESSMENTS AS A KEY APPROACH

For years we have been aware of learner differences. We know well that our students come to us with preferences, interests, and approaches that are commonly referred to as learning styles, modalities, and multiple intelligences. As we engage in varied strategies to accommodate learning preferences we must also make use of similar approaches for student demonstration of learning, accomplishment, and mastery of key outcomes.

Differentiating instruction as we engage learners acknowledges their "input" needs toward generating long-term memory. The same holds true for student production of their evidence of learning outcomes. As we provide opportunities for students to demonstrate their accomplishments, we must consider a variety of ways in which they might produce such evidence. Thus, our approaches to assessment need to reflect the same respect for "output" venues as we provide for "input" methods.

The table on the following page provides a general outline of unit outcomes, separated by type of evidence:

Level 1 **Knowledge**

Level 2 **Performance Tasks or Skills**

Level 3 **Application of Understanding.**

## Differentiated Evidence *&* Assessment

**Students may choose to exhibit their competence with identified key learning elements through a combination of components:**

- Level 1 **Knowledge**
- Level 2 **Performance Tasks or Skills**
- Level 3 **Application of Understanding**

| KNOWLEDGE | PERFORMANCE TASKS OR SKILLS | APPLICATION OF UNDERSTANDING |
|---|---|---|
| What assessment would provide evidence of success with **key knowledge**? | What assessment would provide evidence of success with **key knowledge, key performance tasks, or skills**? | What applied assessment would provide evidence of success with **key knowledge, skills, concepts, and understandings**? |
| Level 1 | Level 2 | Level 3 |
| Assignments and activities at this level, though well done, do not constitute fully *engaged or applied* understanding. Thus, exemplary work in this domain is what we term as "flat" or one-dimensional. We must require learners to go beyond the assimilation, organization, and recitation of information in order to quality for a high grade. | Assignments and activities at this level require that students put the knowledge they have learned to use. They must demonstrate or perform a task that applies the information in a purposeful manner to a real-life, personal or workplace circumstance. This level transfers key learning into other disciplines and/or practices beyond the content of the curriculum. | Assignments and activities at this level cause learners to integrate key knowledge, skills, and understandings into reality. They engage in a workplace, community, or other endeavor that applies the understandings in an actual existing context. This level extends application and understanding to deeper, more integrated circumstances. |

**Students may elect a variety of ways to exhibit their learning of identified, key components:**

- It is appropriate that Level 1 knowledge components would have less weighted value toward a grade than Level 2 performance components ~ and that level 3 applications would carry the most weighted value.

- A rubric would be developed to ascertain the necessary amount of work required in each level to achieve a desired grade or outcome.

| Level 1 | Level 2 | Level 3 |
|---|---|---|
| The student selects a level of involvement from those offered by the teacher that demonstrates the **student's awareness and understanding of the content,** but does not extend that learning to applications. | The student selects a level of involvement from those offered by the teacher that might include generating a thesis statement about the topic contrasting the **related issues and linking them to real-world applications.** | The student selects a level of involvement from those offered by the teacher, identifying a local or regional situation to apply the knowledge to and generate a plan to **integrate key learnings into the improvement, or resolution of an actual issue.** |
| **Example** | **Example** | **Example** |
| Write a paper explaining multiple and varied components of the unit on the targeted area of learning. | Create a brochure that explains major components and informs a specific audience about essential facts and ideas regarding the targeted area of learning that is selected from real-world circumstances. | Get involved with a local agency that is engaged with the targeted area of learning to apply the knowledge in a real setting. |

**See page 37 and Appendix G, beginning on page 117 for additional explanations leading to Level 3 assignments and assessments.**

TEACHER
GUIDE

## Questions to Ask about Assessment Practices and Their Use in the Class

It is vital for teachers to self-assess. Asking a few pertinent questions about the impact of the class as it relates to student applications in real contexts is important to the process of assuring relevant engagement.

### Questions for Teacher:

- How will you know students have mastered key knowledge, skills, or understandings?

- How will you know how successful your approaches or assignments are in helping students master the key learning outcomes of the class?

- What feedback would be beneficial (along the way) to ensure students are progressing with their mastery of key learning outcomes of the class?

- What options will students be afforded to demonstrate their mastery of key learning outcomes of the class?

- What key knowledge and understandings are assessed intermittently and formatively?

- What key knowledge, skills, or understandings are students aware of at the beginning?

Feedback must be timely and unambiguous. It must be diagnostic in nature... it is necessary to establish learning goals and improve achievement outcomes. Administrators that encourage teachers to collect, organize, and evaluate school and classroom data to inform their practice can help improve a school.

"Educators who want to ensure student learning must make use of formative assessment and feedback. Formative assessments are standards-based but have as their sole purpose student learning; There are no immediate consequences for poor performance ~ thus no high stakes. These are designed only to support learning."

Charlotte Danielson, 2002-2003.

- Within an identified subject or class, where do we need to direct our attention to improve outcomes?

- Where do the greatest number of students struggle or fail within the larger domains?

- Which data, well analyzed, can help us understand the impact of our teaching practices?

- Which data, well analyzed, can help us improve student learning?

## Questions for Students:

Feedback from students is also a source of important information for teachers. Obtaining student input is a tool to guide instructional decisions and to considering adjustments for assuring meaningful applications to the field and workplace.

- Attention to what area might be helpful to improve your outcomes?

- What type of items or activities were most frequently challenging to you?

- What key knowledge and understandings were frequently re-assessed?

- What formative (non-graded) feedback was provided that helped you understand in an ongoing manner ~ rather than for grades?

- Is it clear to you what your future needs are in this content area to improve your learning?

**KEY RESOURCES**
See
Bibliography
for Additional
Information

Black, Paul & Wiliam, Dylan. "Inside the Black Box: Raising Standards Through Classroom Assessment"

Black, Paul & Wiliam, Dylan. "Assessment and Classroom Learning"

Donegan, Billie, et. al. *Coaching Reluctant Learners*

Stiggins, Rick. "Assessment Crisis: The Absence of Assessment FOR Learning"

Stiggins, Rick. "Assessment, Student Confidence, and School Success"

**See Appendix D, page 113 and Appendix G, beginning on page 117 for additional Student to Student Interaction information.**

## Chapter **FOUR**

# NEW PARADIGM ~ Where Does This All Lead?

## Curriculum and Development

Implementing this engaging approach to teaching requires new curriculum and unit development processes for educators. The new vision of the role of the teacher as the facilitator of learning requires creating a culture of continuous learning that is flexible, student-centered, and collaborative. The notion that learners must have the opportunity to reflect on their own experiences and research how the new information connects to their own situation is critical.

Engaging instruction is an orientation associated with emphasis on the social and political context of learning. This view of teaching and learning is reflected in participatory curricula, in which learners themselves identify problems, and through cycles of reflections and action, seek solutions to shared challenges. If learners are provided with an opportunity to identify key issues that are relevant to them, they themselves can identify goals for what they want to be able to do. Within this learner-centered framework, it becomes the instructors task to work with learners to move toward their goals, and to facilitate the skills they need to achieve further success.

**EDUCATOR DEVELOPMENT NEEDS**

The challenges for current educators are formidable. Never before have our institutions been asked to ensure that students achieve publicly defined outcomes of learning, and never before have we been faced with such a diversity of learners and learner needs.

If we are serious about addressing this dilemma, then we need to recognize that high quality teaching practices are essential to impact student learning for higher quality outcomes. Teachers must take the lead in transforming our classrooms to meet the challenges of life long learning. Instructors need to think about the teaching and learning process, and focus on key, central outcomes that are connected to ongoing student performance. Educators no longer have the mere luxury of covering a text-based curriculum, but must engage diverse learners ~ empowering them to construct their own knowledge and develop their talents in an effective way. This means a shift in the delivery of classroom instruction that incorporates real-life application of learning, embeds performance based assessments, and provides opportunity for student choice. Faculty must reconstruct their role, work within new structures for organizing learning (not teaching), develop new skills, and instruct as they never have instructed before.

**WHAT FACULTY SHOULD KNOW AND BE ABLE TO DO?**

- Facilitate the learning that places the student at the center

- Set high expectations and articulate clear outcomes for the learners

- Demand content and instruction that ensures student achievement of the identified learning outcomes

- Create a culture of continuous learning that embraces opportunities for supporting innovation and entrepreneurial experiences

- Use multiple resources and tools to assess and apply instructional improvement

- Actively engage the community, and create "real-world" opportunities for students to practice their learning.

**THE NEW PARADIGM**

As this new paradigm in education unfolds, we must embrace an evolving way of doing business that focuses on outcome-based designs with accountability for results. We must leave behind the old school of thought that focuses on teaching as a process of delivering important curriculum. Now, we must focus on teaching as the process through which students achieve important knowledge along with the proficiency to perform targeted tasks as a result of their learning experience.

This paradigm highlights the importance of understanding the new research on how we (today's learner) learn as well as employing instructional strategies and activities that develop higher order thinking skills and the ability to apply knowledge and understanding to existing work situations and life challenges.

Clearly, these new requirements challenge teachers to acquire new skills, develop curriculum through a new framework of thought, and in many instances, adopt new orientations to the process of orchestrating the teaching ~ learning intersection.

## Proactive Instruction

| TRADITIONAL Paradigm | NEW Paradigm |
|---|---|
| Focus on student behavior | Focus on student learning |
| Focus on content or knowledge control | Focus on effective teaching practices |
| Judgment based on personal philosophy and teaching style | Assessments based on evidence of student learning |
| Focus on text outline to guide instructional plan | Focus on and design backward from identified outcomes |
| One-size fits-all unit of study requirements | Student choice to demonstrate evidence of success |
| Power or authority supersedes | Research-based best practices are the basis for expertise |
| Each assignment is a discrete event | Assignments are linked to specific outcomes |

EMERGING
CLASSROOM
PRACTICES

- Have faculty guiding student inquiry

- Pose problem situations related to real life issues

- Provide a variety of opportunities for students to explore and confront concepts and situations over time

- Organize learning around big picture issues rather than fragmented units of information

- Use multiple sources of information rather than a single text

- Have students work together to enhance the learning process

- Use multiple forms of assessment to gather evidence of the learning.

**See Appendix A, beginning on page 101 for additional Curriculum and Development information.**

## A Framework to Support the New Paradigm

OVERVIEW   Participatory educators suggest that in order for learners to develop skills for addressing challenges in their own lives as well as their field of study, they must have an opportunity to identify those issues. Inviting learners to provide input in planning, in the on-going development of curriculum, as well as in classroom activities is at the core of this design frame. Students whose prior knowledge and experiences are valued tend to get the most from their learning efforts. As learners expand their repertoire of knowledge and behaviors, and are given the opportunity to monitor their own progress, new possibilities and goals often come into view.

Guiding questions for planning:

- What current ideas in the field are important for the learners to examine?

- What are the primary concerns of the learners in your class?

- How are the learners invited to express their concerns and interests, both in the planning process and throughout the unit of study, as well as inside and outside of class time?

- What community resources are available to support the learning and overall classroom experience?

- How will learners be offered the opportunity to choose which learning and assessment strategies are most important ~ and perhaps most impacting ~ to them?

- At what points will learners have an opportunity to set and re-evaluate their own learning goals, and monitor their progress toward them?

- How is the role of existing knowledge recognized in the construction of new knowledge?

- When do learners have an opportunity to share their experiences with others regarding the unit of study?

- How is essential learning made available to other learners in and across other units of study?

**FRAMEWORK & INTRODUCTION TO THE METAPHOR**

The following five-column concept map (page 78) is designed to establish the connections between the framework for a unit of study, and the process of undertaking a metaphorical journey (page 79 ~ follows the framework) from one place to a desired location. Organizing successful learning opportunities for today's students has many parallels to planning and building components of traveling from one place to a designated destination.

**A blank concept map of the framework is included in Appendix B, beginning on page 103 for your use as a worksheet for generating important elements of a unit of study.**

## UNIT OF STUDY FRAMEWORK: Constructing Successful Learning Opportunities for Today's Students

**ELABORATION** FIVE-STEP COURSE DEVELOPMENT FRAMEWORK

| Relevance Levels | Step **1**<br>UNIT OF STUDY, CONCEPTS, & CONTENT | Step **2**<br>DEVELOPING CONTEXT | Step **3**<br>"ROLL OUT" PACING | Step **4**<br>APPROACH, PROCESS, & ACTIVITY | Step **5**<br>ASSESSMENT & EVIDENCE OF SUCCESS |
|---|---|---|---|---|---|
| **Applications** | **Grade or Department**<br>Each unit of study must identify key learning components the learner will need to know and be able to do. | **Each Key Component is Embedded in a Context**<br>Each key component has a context in which purpose and meaning are evidenced by the learner. | **Develop a Purposeful Order**<br>Sequence the key learnings as to when learners will encounter them. | **Determine Strategies**<br>Select strategies to encourage engagement: applied learning, choice, interaction, and assessment. | **Quality Assurance**<br>Gather credible feedback by generating data on summative assessment, formative feedback, and instructional approaches. |
| **Key Learning Components** | Identify key learnings of the unit (knowledge, skills, and understandings). | Ground the unit's main purposes in today's applications. | Plan the unit of study by pacing knowledge, skills, and understandings across the allotted timeline. | Determine strategies to use in your instruction that incorporate the essentials of applied learning, choice, interaction, and feedback/assessment. | Gather feedback about learner understanding and the effectiveness of teacher approaches. |
| **Overarching Questions** | What major areas will the learner need to know, be able to do and understand as a result of the unit of study? | Where are key learning components relevant (active) in today's world? | What sequence will be used to pace out key learnings for students to tackle? | How will you engage students? How will your strategies ensure that the students apply key learning components? | What summative evidence is needed? What formative feedback is needed? When? |

**METAPHOR** PLANNING A TRIP TO A SPECIFIC DESTINATION

| | Step **1** | Step **2** | Step **3** | Step **4** | Step **5** |
|---|---|---|---|---|---|
| **Relevance Levels** | **UNIT OF STUDY, CONCEPTS, & CONTENT** | **DEVELOPING CONTEXT** | **"ROLL OUT" PACING** | **APPROACH, PROCESS, & ACTIVITY** | **ASSESSMENT & EVIDENCE OF SUCCESS** |
| **Applications** | **Grade or Department**<br><br>Successful student accomplishment of the journey (key elements of travel) of the overall unit (trip) and the identified elements to be learned. | **Each Key Component is Embedded in a Context**<br><br>Personal applications?<br><br>Purpose of travel?<br><br>Important components of travel?<br><br>Multiple routes to take to get there? | **Develop a Purposeful Order**<br><br>Develop a travel plan and map for the journey that accomplishes intended outcomes and builds understandings regarding travel. | **Determine Strategies**<br><br>Who are the travelers?<br><br>What differences, preferences, and experiences do they bring? | **Quality Assurance**<br><br>Maintain a personal log of the journey.<br><br>Intermittently track key learning for mode of transport, route, stops along the way, etc.<br><br>Successful adjustments are made along the way. |
| **Key Learning Components** | | ▪ **WEATHER**   ▪ **TRANSPORTATION**<br>▪ **ROUTE**   ▪ **ACCOMMODATIONS**<br>▪ **TIME**   ▪ **OTHER IMPORTANT FACTORS?**<br>▪ **COSTS** | | | |
| **Overarching Questions** | What knowledge, skills, or understandings will the learner need to know regarding travel? | Where are the key components of travel relevant in today's world? | What order or sequence of travel makes sense?<br><br>By what criteria? | What will the needs of the travelers be?<br><br>Are there accommodations or alternatives that would promote their collective successes? | By what criteria was the journey successful?<br><br>Did mid-journey adjustments make sense? |

| Step **1** | ELABORATION & QUESTIONS | METAPHOR:  PLANNING A TRIP TO A SPECIFIC DESTINATION | Template Reference: p. 102. |
|---|---|---|---|
| Relevance Level<br>**UNIT OF STUDY, CONCEPTS, &<br>CONTENT** | **KEY LEARNING COMPONENTS**<br>- Example: Literary Devices in Poetry, Main Ideas in Paragraphs, Strategic Events of WWI, Elements that Form Communities, Inequalities, Attributes of Insects, Requirements of Plant Life, etc. | **KEY METAPHOR COMPONENTS**<br>- The teacher must focus on successful student accomplishment of the journey (key elements of travel) of the overall unit (trip) and the identified elements to be learned.<br>- The planners (students) need to consider many essential items prior to taking a trip.<br>- Example: Weather, Route, Time, Costs, Transportation, Accommodations, etc. | **Column ONE**<br>* Identify General Concepts and Understandings |
| Application<br>**GRADE OR DEPARTMENT**<br>**Each unit of study must have its key learning components identified.** | **OVERARCHING QUESTIONS**<br>- What major big ideas or knowledge will the learner need to know as a result of this unit of study?<br>- What major skills or abilities will the learner need to be able to do as a result of this unit of study?<br>- What major understandings will the learner have as a result of this unit of study?<br>- How will identified key learnings be articulated to the student prior to the beginning of the unit of study? | **ESSENTIAL LEARNING COMPONENTS**<br>- **WEATHER** What will we encounter along the way? How much flexibility in our travels will we need to allow for?<br>- **ROUTE** Which path will provide the best outcomes? Based on which needs or criteria?<br>- **TIME** How much time will we need? What factors will influence this?<br>- **COSTS** What investments or contributions will travelers need to make?<br>- **TRANSPORTATION** Are there multiple modes of travel ~ or ways of getting there?<br>- **ACCOMMODATIONS** What criteria will we use to select the lodging? To meet which needs?<br>- **OTHER IMPORTANT FACTORS?** | **Column TWO**<br>* Identify Key Learning Targets of this Unit<br>* Identify Knowledge, Skills, or Abilities Required for Success |

| Step **2** | ELABORATION & QUESTIONS | METAPHOR: PLANNING A TRIP TO A SPECIFIC DESTINATION | Template Reference: p. 102. |
|---|---|---|---|
| Relevance Level<br>**CONTEXT** | KEY LEARNING COMPONENTS<br><br>▪ Ground the unit's main purposes in today's applications. | KEY METAPHOR COMPONENTS<br><br>▪ Review possible personal applications<br><br>▪ Clarify purpose of travel<br><br>▪ Review practicality and clarify important components of travel and its impact(s)<br><br>▪ Consider multiple paths to learning | |
| Application<br>**KEY COMPONENTS EMBEDDED IN CONTEXT**<br><br>**Each key component has a context in which purpose and meaning are developed for or with the learner.** | OVERARCHING QUESTIONS<br><br>▪ Where are the key learning components relevant (active) in today's world?<br><br>▪ What key components of learning in this unit of study are evidenced in today's school, community, workplace, or in the students' lives in general?<br><br>▪ How can the students become engaged in applying the key components to be learned to their personal circumstances (home, school, community, peers, interests)?<br><br> | ESSENTIAL LEARNING COMPONENTS<br><br>▪ **WEATHER** What adjustments may be needed, by whom?<br><br>▪ **ROUTE** Which paths will be viable or of interest for the travelers as each relates to the key learning components?<br><br>▪ **TIME** Which components are fundamental? Which are secondary? How do I ensure the fundamentals are covered or reinforced?<br><br>▪ **COSTS** What investments will travelers need to make (separately, in groups, all)?<br><br>▪ **TRANSPORTATION** What choices will travelers have in *how* they travel? Are there multiple ways to arrive at the destination? Which are viable, to whom?<br><br>▪ **ACCOMMODATIONS** What is required to secure lodging?<br><br>▪ **OTHER IMPORTANT FACTORS?** | |

| Step **3** | ELABORATION *&* QUESTIONS | METAPHOR: PLANNING A TRIP TO A SPECIFIC DESTINATION | Template Reference: p. 102. |
|---|---|---|---|
| Relevance Level<br><br>**"ROLL OUT" PACING** | KEY LEARNING COMPONENTS<br><br>■ Plan the unit of study by pacing knowledge, skills, and understandings across the allotted timeline.<br><br>■ Construct a sequence of classes by parsing out key learnings based on overall unit of study outcomes. | KEY METAPHOR COMPONENTS<br><br>■ Develop a sequence map for the journey that accomplishes target outcomes and builds desired understanding(s)<br><br>■ Identify each major element (route, hazards, etc.) and its outcomes (successful travel)<br><br>■ Organize (mode of travel, weather considerations, etc.) to efficiently and effectively accomplish the goals (arrival at the destination). |  |
| Application<br><br>**DEVELOP A PURPOSEFUL ORDER**<br><br>**Sequence the key learnings and establish the timing for learners to become exposed to them.** | OVERARCHING QUESTIONS<br><br>■ Is there an order that the major understandings need to be introduced and applied by students?<br><br>■ What knowledge or skills must accompany each major understanding?<br><br>■ How much time will it take to get to each sub-location along the journey? | ESSENTIAL LEARNING COMPONENTS<br><br>■ **WEATHER** What affect might unforeseen weather have on the journey?<br><br>■ **ROUTE** What considerations accompany each path?<br><br>■ **TIME** How will I ensure all fundamentals are covered, while providing extended options for travel beyond the primary or fastest route?<br><br>■ **COSTS** What commitment will be required of students for each chosen path?<br><br>■ **TRANSPORTATION** What rate of travel is viable ~ with what requirements? What mid-course check-ups would be helpful?<br><br>■ **ACCOMMODATIONS** What accommodations may accompany each path?<br><br>■ **OTHER IMPORTANT FACTORS?** | ALL Columns<br><br>* This aspect cuts across how each component of the unit will be sequenced, carried out, and assessed. |

| Step **4** | ELABORATION & QUESTIONS | METAPHOR: PLANNING A TRIP TO A SPECIFIC DESTINATION | Template Reference: p. 102. |
|---|---|---|---|
| Relevance Level<br>**APPROACH, PROCESS, & ACTIVITY** | KEY LEARNING COMPONENTS<br><br>■ Determine strategies to use in your instruction that incorporate the essentials of applied learning, choice, interaction, and feedback/assessment. | KEY METAPHOR COMPONENTS<br><br>■ Explore travel applications to arrive at your destination on time, and within your budget<br><br>■ Consider the variety of students you will have in your class (choices, dispositions, experiences, etc.) to do the work (explore alignment of key ideas) and how to help each get his/her components of the journey done well. | |
| Application<br>**DETEREMINE STRATEGIES**<br>**Select strategies to encourage engagement and application: applied learning, choice, interaction, and assessment.** | OVERARCHING QUESTIONS<br><br>■ How will you engage students?<br>■ How will you ensure that the students apply key learning components?<br>■ What activities, assignments, or approaches could you use that would engage students in steps one through three above?<br>■ How will you ensure that the students engage in and construct their own knowledge and understandings as they apply to their personal lives or interests? | ESSENTIAL LEARNING COMPONENTS<br><br>■ **WEATHER** How will students be guided to consider options? What feedback along the way will help students make adjustments?<br>■ **ROUTE** How will students navigate their path? What considerations accompany each route?<br>■ **TIME** How long will each leg take?<br>■ **COSTS** How will each traveler come to understand the level of investment required for each choice?<br>■ **TRANSPORTATION** What modes of transporting oneself are available? What feedback along the way is needed to see that everyone is making reasonable progress?<br>■ **ACCOMMODATIONS** How will the accommodations be selected?<br>■ **OTHER IMPORTANT FACTORS?** | Column FOUR<br><br>* Consider how you will engage the students through the framework of applied learning, interaction, choice, and feedback. |

| Step **5** | ELABORATION & QUESTIONS | METAPHOR: PLANNING A TRIP TO A SPECIFIC DESTINATION | Template Reference: p. 102. |
|---|---|---|---|
| Relevance Level<br><br>**ASSESSMENT &**<br>**EVIDENCE OF**<br>**SUCCESS** | **KEY LEARNING COMPONENTS**<br><br>▪ Gather feedback about learner work and teacher instructional approaches<br><br>▪ Evaluate the success of the learner (as well as your selected instructional approaches and activities) along the way, then also at the end<br><br>▪ What summative evidence is needed?<br><br>▪ What formative feedback is needed? | **KEY METAPHOR COMPONENTS**<br><br>▪ Travelers maintain a personal log documenting their journey, describing experiences, learning component, and assisting in the evaluation<br><br>▪ Ongoing feedback is needed to confirm that each key learning for travel has taken place (mode, route, stops along the way, etc.)<br><br>▪ Adjustments are made along the way (reservations, route, etc.) until key learnings (successful travel) are completed to satisfaction | **Column THREE**<br><br>* Before instruction begins, all assessments are formulated in deference to the key learnings identified in Columns ONE and TWO. |
| Application<br><br>**QUALITY**<br>**ASSURANCE**<br><br>**Gather credible feedback by gathering data on instructional approaches, summative assessment, and formative feedback.** | **OVERARCHING QUESTIONS**<br><br>▪ What final summative indicators will you look for at the conclusion of the unit of study, and provide to or discuss with students at the beginning?<br><br>▪ How are they tied to the key components of learning you have identified?<br><br>▪ What formative frequent feedback (about key components of learning) *TO STUDENTS* would be useful to support student learning?<br><br>▪ What feedback do YOU need about students? When (at what intervals)?<br><br>▪ What feedback do you need about the strategies and assignments you are using? When? | **ESSENTIAL LEARNING COMPONENTS**<br><br>▪ **WEATHER** What provisions for alternatives are in the journey plan?<br><br>▪ **ROUTE** What elements are essential for executing a successful journey?<br><br>▪ **TIME** What fundamentals are parts of the journey? How are they evidenced?<br><br>▪ **COSTS** To what extent will the travelers embrace the journey and its options?<br><br>▪ **TRANSPORTATION** How did the type of travel chosen impact the journey?<br><br>▪ **ACCOMMODATIONS** Did accommodations fit established criteria?<br><br>▪ **OTHER IMPORTANT FACTORS?** | |

## Implementing the Framework

**Step ONE**

### Unit of Study Concept *&* Content Level

Template Reference: p. 102.

ANALYSIS OF TASKS AND FRAMEWORK OVERVIEW

Once the essential outcomes have been determined, the concepts and specific skills that the student will need to meet the goals are identified. Keeping in mind where the class or unit of study fits in the curriculum will ensure that, whenever necessary, requisite concepts and skills will be reviewed. Initial baseline assessments are used to determine student needs and capacity.

**Key Content Knowledge**

Can you clearly identify the new knowledge that needs to be learned by the student in this content area?

**Key Performance Components**

Can you clearly identify the skills that need to be learned as a result of this class or unit of study?

**Key Concepts**

Can you clearly identify what the students need to *understand* with respect to big ideas and general concepts as a result of this class/unit of study?

**Action** ▪ Make a list for each item above. Be sure to only list (keep) the essential elements of each. You will arrange the items chronologically later on.

Column ONE

* Key Learning Targets

* Key Learning Targets

Column TWO

* Overarching Learning Targets

Template Reference: p. 102.

**ESSENTIAL QUESTIONS**

1. Have you identified all essential "know," "able to do" and "understandings" of the class or unit of study?

2. Are they organized in a manner that would be clear and understandable to the students?

## Step **TWO**

*"Asking questions of people [others with expertise or knowledge in the content area]... who should know, often isn't enough. It doesn't matter how smart they are, how well they know the product or the opportunities. It doesn't matter how many astute questions you ask.*

*If you're not in the jungle, you're not going to know the tiger."*

"The Art of Innovation,"
Kelly, 2001.

## Contextual Relevance as the Link to Student Meaning by Gathering Meaningful Resources

Template Reference: p. 102.

OVERVIEW **Current Sources**

Although traditional textbooks are important resources to lesson or unit development, engaging students with current issues that have meaning to them must be the anchor of the design. This era of information explosion and instant communication, presents an opportunity for classrooms today to connect students with the relevant application of their content under study. Technology has given faculty and students the capacity to examine the innovations being explored and the questions and challenges ahead. The instructor develops contextual relevance for each of the key "know, able to do, and conceptual understandings" of the class/unit of study by scanning current resources.

**Key Content Knowledge**

Where does the key knowledge surface in current events, locations, community, or workplaces today?

Column TWO

* Overarching Learning Targets

* Overarching Learning Targets

**Key Performance Components**

How is the key knowledge being performed (put into use or applied) in current events, locations, community, or workplaces today?

Template Reference: p. 102.

**Key Concepts** What essential understandings are being applied or developed in current events, locations, community, or workplaces today?

Locating this type of information can be found in resources such as: articles, websites, local happenings, videos, texts, specific companies, field site visits, workplace task analyses, etc.

**Action**
- Identify places, sources, industries, community events that are taking place RIGHT NOW ~ that rely on the knowledge, skills, and understandings that this class/unit of study intends learners to acquire and put to use.

- Make a list of such resources.

- Students will use these leads as vehicles for your assignments, projects, and other opportunities for demonstrating proficiencies.

**ESSENTIAL QUESTIONS**
1. Where do the key knowledge and skills show up in the world? Life? The community? School? The workforce?

2. Where are the major concepts in play today?

Column ONE

* Key Learning Targets

Column FOUR

* Strategies to Consider in Student Achievement

## Step **THREE**

# Rolling Out the Unit of Study ~ Pacing Lessons

Template Reference: p. 102.

**OVERVIEW**    The instructor "rolls out" the unit of study into a sequence of study across the number of weeks allotted. Attention is given to the order of knowledge, skills, concepts, and understandings that will ensure students have the opportunity to develop the learning capacity they need to be successful. Higher order thinking skills are the new basic skills and are embedded throughout the unit of study roll-out.

**Key Content Knowledge**    What key knowledge is foundational (needed first)?

Can you identify the chronology of information that students will access/encounter so that you can map these on to the unit of study schedule?

**Key Performance Components**    What key performance skills are needed, and when?

Can you identify the chronology of skills/capabilities that students will access/encounter so that you can map these on to the unit of study sequence?

**Key Concepts**    What essential understandings (concepts) will be required? When?

Can you identify the chronology of concepts that students will access/encounter so that you can map these on to the unit of study sequence?

Column TWO & THREE
* Overarching Learning Targets and Evidence of Student Achievement

* Overarching Learning Targets and Evidence of Student Achievement

* Overarching Learning Targets and Evidence of Student Achievement

Template Reference: p. 102.

**Action** ▪ Create "placeholders" in each scheduled class meeting for key knowledge, performance skills, and concept understandings, as you see them relating to the chronology of the sequence of lessons to be coordinated over consecutive weeks of the unit of study.

**ESSENTIAL QUESTIONS** 1. What sequence of exposure to knowledge, skills and understandings will best help students acquire desired capacities?

Step **FOUR**

## The Approach: Process *&* Activity Development

Template Reference: p. 102.

**OVERVIEW**

Explore instructional practices and strategies that will engage students to construct meaning regarding key learning outcomes. Identify materials and resources that students can access to build the capacity to apply their knowledge, skills, and understandings.

**Essential Application Questions**

What strategies will help learners to be engaged, regarding key learnings?

What assignments will provide students with the opportunity to apply key learnings?

What provisions will you make for students to engage in designing (choice) components of their work?

How will students work together? On what items?

What intermittent feedback will help you know how students are doing, with respect to their acquisition of key learnings?

**Action**

▪ Identify ways to engage students in: applied learning for relevance; student choice for empowerment and meaning; interaction with peers or others; and feedback that informs progress throughout the unit of study ~ especially on identified key learnings. Locate essential resource options for students to consider.

Column FOUR

\* Strategies to Consider in Student Achievement

Column THREE

\* Before instruction begins, all assessments are formulated in deference to the key learnings identified in Columns ONE and TWO.

Column FOUR

\* Strategies to Consider in Student Achievement

Template Reference:  p. 102.

**ESSENTIAL QUESTIONS**

1. Where will students be engaged with applied learning (relevance) opportunities?

2. Where will students be engaged with opportunities for choice?

3. Where will students be engaged with opportunities for interaction with peers? With others outside the classroom? With people who are using the knowledge, skills or concepts being studied?

4. What resources will you need to support student engagement for meaning and application?

Step **FIVE**

## Assessment *&* Evidence of Success

Template Reference: p. 102.

OVERVIEW

The exchange of ideas and information is crucial to the learning process. Feedback is one of the most important vehicles available to secure and retain learning. Both formal assessment activities, as well as more formative opportunities for providing evidence of accomplishment and success, are vital guides for the teacher and student to use in making adjustments along the way.

**Essential Application Questions**

Student Adjustments for Learning Outcomes: What feedback will you provide and when, in order to assure that students are "on-track" and mastering key learnings?

Teacher Adjustments for Learning Outcomes: What feedback do you need and when, to know how well your strategies and assignments are working to help students with key learnings?

What type(s) of feedback are best suited to the desired unit of study outcomes you have identified?

**Action**

- Identify knowledge, performance, and concept feedback that will be beneficial to bolster learning outcomes, at designated intervals throughout the unit of study.

- Identify and form all assessments, prior to the start of class.

- Make all assessment types, formats, and intentions known to students.

- Be sure to develop some assessment processes that provide student choice, on how to demonstrate learning outcomes.

Column THREE

* Before instruction begins, all assessments are formulated in deference to the key learnings identified in Columns ONE and TWO.

**Chapter FIVE**

# ADMINISTRATOR'S ROLE
## IN SUPPORTING AND SUSTAINING THE ENGAGEMENT OF TODAY'S STUDENTS

*"The Concise Oxford Dictionary, 10th Edition (2001), offers a simple definition of intelligence: 'the ability to acquire and apply knowledge and skills.' In this sense, Einstein experimenting with the space-time continuum, a teenager playing an electronic game, and an infant toying with blocks all exhibit intelligence."*

Reeves, 2006.

Added to the items in the quote to the left would be a teacher working to apply strategies, brain research, and rigorous curricular challenges with a group of diverse learners. This would be an exhibition of intelligence as well. In all cases, intelligent behavior benefits from assistance, guidance, and collaborative efforts.

Applying the ideas contained in the framework of this book can be done in isolation (many attempt such). However, it is the exchanges between educators that generate the understandings of nuance, the adjustments for certain learner needs, and the breakthroughs in mastering approaches that serve many, many students.

The administrator must take part in this process. S/he is essential to the support needed for teachers to convene, communicate ideas and concerns, and to experiment with facets of this framework. They need not do/use all of the ideas contained in this book ~ but can start at any place, with any idea, strategy or approach. Teacher success will be exponentially greater if faculty work as partners to uncover the subtle, yet pertinent shifts in perspective that will unleash their students' interests and efforts.

It is the leader's role to ensure that efforts are encouraged, implemented, and monitored.. We all struggle with new notions. Providing opportunities to work with them to fruition is key to the transition. Thus, this work is hardly the domain of the classroom practitioner alone.

Two prominent questions frame the role of instructional leaders:

1. How do leaders engage their staff in a manner that will help to initiate the undertakings this book outlines?

2. Once initiated, what can a leader do to help sustain effective practices?

Guidance comes from both the workplace and schools.

Thomas Guskey offers five levels that encompass the effects of professional development activities and embedded practices. He suggests that as we engage in efforts to improve our teaching practices as a means to increasing learner performance that we will benefit from examining the path of learning for the adults. His levels are:

**Level 1**    participant's reactions (day of ~ did you like it?)

**Level 2**    participant's learning (day of ~ what knowledge or skills have you gained?)

Don Kirkpatrick outlines four levels of evaluation of the impact of efforts to develop new practices from training opportunities. His four levels are as follows:

Level 1    the learner's initial reaction to the training program (day of)

Level 2    the learning that has occurred as a result of the training (day of)

Level 3    changes in behavior on the job as a result of the training program (ongoing)

Level 4    the results of the training program as it affects the company's bottom line (over a designated period of time).

**Level 3** organizational support and change (day of ~ is the intended learning aligned with our mission? Is there time and resource for reflection and follow up? )

**Level 4** participants' use of learnings (has the activity made a difference in practice? Is there evidence of the skills/knowledge acquired being put into use?)

**Level 5** Student learning outcomes: Is there evidence of improvement in the intended student learning outcomes (targeted) from the activity?

A traditional process of evaluation (i.e. consult, visit, observe and conference with the teacher) can be quite time consuming. Many administrators would openly (or at least off the record) admit that the impact of the process falls short of what might be desired. Many teachers would corroborate administrative sentiments articulating a lack of purposeful outcomes from the process. Thoughtful feedback regarding instructional strengths and areas of concern are most helpful in assisting teachers to be the best they can be. Yet, often the process is diluted by generalities and unclear foci. Both of these frustrating deficiencies can be addressed with the straightforward approach illustrated below.

As new strategies and approaches are undertaken by staff, align the professional learning opportunity with an invitation for built in follow-up. The sequence of activities might go like this:

1. Before professional development (PD) begins, identify the student and/or adult learning need(s) that the activity targets (i.e. what prompted us to engage in this endeavor? What do we hope to be the result of having undertaken this process?)

2. Have the providers or leaders of the PD process articulated the components of the process that align with each identified student or adult learning need?

3. As the PD "program" is taking place, stop at intermittent junctures and ask participants to identify which learning need is being addressed by the strategy or idea being offered. Have participants work in pairs, grade level teams, or by department to discuss the feasibility of the strategy, how to implement it, when, and with what adjustments.

   a. Do this for each new strategy or category of ideas under consideration

4. Near the end of the allotted time, have participants once again meet to discuss:

   a. Which of the strategies or ideas do you feel are most likely to:

      i. be successful with the students ~ with respect to the learning targets?

      ii. be used by both of you (pairs); all of you (team or department)

5. Have the pairs, teams, or departments decide on two or three key strategies they would agree to practice on

6. Have the pairs, teams, or departments determine who they will work with (no one works alone) to plan, implement, and discuss the impact of each strategy

7. Determine how successes, frustrations and questions regarding each selected strategy will be communicated to all involved

8. Ask each participant to invite their supervisor to observe when a new strategy is being attempted (either first time or in subsequent times). This way:

   a. The observation is focused on an intended learning need

   b. Student response to the selected strategy can be documented and discussed for adjustment, for future use or put aside in favor of a more promising strategy

   c. Successes can be shared with others by the teacher or the supervisor ~ based on a first-hand experience! When parties collaborate to explore the impact of a new idea or strategy with respect to student learning outcomes, everybody gains. Collectively, involved professionals benefit from each other's points of view, experiences, and ideas for modification to help everyone be more successful with a strategy that clearly links with improved student performance outcomes.

The dialogue that can emanate from such a process can turn difficult circumstances into collaborative discussions focused on improving student performance.

Chapter **SIX**

# CONCLUSION

The challenge of transforming our classrooms is a priority in this changing educational climate. Policy and system leaders must recognize the need to examine present practices and support these new issues for the expanding, global economy. But it is our belief that the teacher who interacts closest to the learner makes the difference, one step at a time.

As we have heard so many times before, change is inevitable. It is our hope that you will embrace change as a mean of continuous improvement in this field of learning, as it relates to the teaching profession. The framework presented in this book can be applied to any content area and to any existing developed unit sequence. It does take commitment and perseverance to implement the approach, practice the concepts, and assess the areas in need of improvement. Once achieved, you will never view the teaching/learning intersection quite the same.

Reaching out to each student and engaging them in the learning is what teaching is all about. Who knows ~ the next Albert Einstein may be sitting right before you!

You can make a difference!

# APPENDICES BY CATEGORY

**APPENDIX A**

## Unit of Study Template

The Unit of Study Template on the following page is intended to provide an at a glance summary of important items that need to be articulated for a unit of study.

Use it as a quick reference for a chapter, unit, or other learning segment. It also doubles as a handout so that students can see the focus of upcoming studies.

Reference links for this template have been placed on the UNIT OF STUDY FRAMEWORK on pages 78-84 and in Appendix B.

## UNIT OF STUDY TEMPLATE: Learning Targets, Evidence of Achievement, *&* Strategies

| COLUMN ONE<br>**Overarching Learning Targets** | COLUMN TWO<br>**Key Learning Targets for this Unit of Study** | COLUMN THREE<br>**Evidence of Student Achievement** | COLUMN FOUR<br>**Strategies to Consider in Helping Students Achieve** |
|---|---|---|---|
| What general concepts and understandings are expected as a result of this unit of study? | What key <u>knowledge</u> is essential to this unit?<br><br><br>What key <u>skills or abilities</u> are essential to this unit?<br><br><br>In order to be successful at acquiring the above, what <u>requisite</u> knowledge or skills are needed? | How will you know what students have learned? When?<br><br>**Summative Assessments**<br>Measure for each item in columns one and two:<br>▪ KNOW<br>▪ BE ABLE TO DO<br>▪ UNDERSTAND<br><br>**Formative Assessments**<br>Measure for each item:<br>▪ KNOW<br>▪ BE ABLE TO DO<br>▪ UNDERSTAND<br><br>**Feedback**<br>Measure for each requisite item: | What <u>strategies</u> make sense, based on the material to be learned and the student's need?<br><br>As you consider strategies, look them over to assure there are elements of the framework (not in each strategy, but overall).<br><br>A  Relevant Applied Learning<br><br>B  Student Interaction<br><br>C  Student Choice-Option<br><br>D  Intermittent Formative Feedback *&* Evidence of Learning |

2005, Modified from Greenleaf Learning Documents.

## APPENDIX B

# Unit of Study Framework

The following three pages are intended to be a working document ~ a worksheet for instructors applying the six-step process outlined in this book, on pages 78-84. Please make copies of this template, as needed.

## UNIT OF STUDY FRAMEWORK: Constructing Successful Learning Opportunities for Today's Students

| **PART ONE** Prior to Instruction, please consider all of the following 5 steps below: | **PART TWO** After considering all 5 steps on the left, factor in the key learning components to focus on each step of the process. |
|---|---|
| Step **1**<br>Relevance Level<br>**UNIT OF STUDY, CONCEPTS, & CONTENT**<br><br>Application<br>**GRADE OR DEPARTMENT**<br><br>**A task-analysis for each unit of study must have its key learning components identified.** | KEY LEARNING COMPONENTS: |
| Step **2**<br>Relevance Level<br>**CONTEXT**<br><br>Application<br>**KEY COMPONENTS EMBEDDED IN CONTEXT**<br><br>**Each key component has a context in which purpose and meaning are developed for or with the learner.** | KEY LEARNING COMPONENTS: |

**PART ONE** Prior to Instruction, please consider all of the following 5 steps below:

**PART TWO** After considering all 5 steps on the left, factor in the key learning components to focus on each step of the process.

Step **3**

Relevance Level
**"ROLL OUT" PACING**

Application
**DEVELOP A PURPOSEFUL ORDER**

Sequence the key learnings and establish the timing of when learners will encounter them.

KEY LEARNING COMPONENTS:

Step **4**

Relevance Level
**APPROACH, PROCESS, & ACTIVITY**

Application
**DETEREMINE STRATEGIES**

Select strategies to encourage engagement: applied learning, choice, interaction, and assessment.

KEY LEARNING COMPONENTS:

**PART ONE** Prior to instruction, please consider all of the following 5 steps below:

**PART TWO** After considering all 5 steps on the left, factor in the key learning components to focus on each step of the process.

Step **5**

Relevance Level
**ASSESSMENT** *&* **EVIDENCE OF SUCCESS**

Application
**QUALITY ASSURANCE**

**Gather credible feedback by gathering data on the effectiveness of instructional approaches, summative assessment, and formative feedback.**

KEY LEARNING COMPONENTS:

**APPENDIX C**

# Brain Sciences & Learning

## The Road to Capacity Building in Long-Term Memory and Recall

Basic levels of processing in the brain are commonly discussed at three levels (see the illustration that follows). The initial level (bottom) is sensory. At this level, inputs enter the brain via the senses, and the brain previews these in quick fashion. Most are immediately discarded (the fact that a blue car has passed by is hardly as important as the familiar colleague walking in our direction). While we "take in" millions of inputs, most is not important to us, thus we readily dismiss it.

A small fraction of inputs are elevated to the middle level or "working memory," the "desktop" metaphor for actively processing inputs. This refers to brain activity that is processed longer, and in more depth. Connections to meaning, patterns, or a link to other previously known items are sought. This in no way insures adequate learning, but does constitute additional thought, interest, or attention to the input for organization, categorization, understanding, responding in class, writing a paper, or for some other purposeful activity.

Working memory activity is the predecessor to long-term memory (LTM). Though some things may achieve long-term status more quickly through an emotionally charged episode or novelty, the vast amount of inputs require more substantive processing, prior to semi- or permanent memory formation. When the brain "pulls" prior experience, knowledge, or ideas from what is already residing in long-term memory (the metaphoric storage "barn"), and considers new information or ideas in relation to what is already known or stored, the chances of the new inputs being incorporated into memory for a longer duration increase dramatically.

Our goal in teaching is to create conditions and learning opportunities in which learners are more likely to make greater attempts at sufficient processing. Outcomes of improved understanding, application, and long-term memory and recall are then expected. The illustration on the next page may be useful as a conceptual graphic to consider, in thinking about this process.

## Memory Formation Occurs as a Multiple Level Process

### The Barn

Long-Term Memory Processing Level

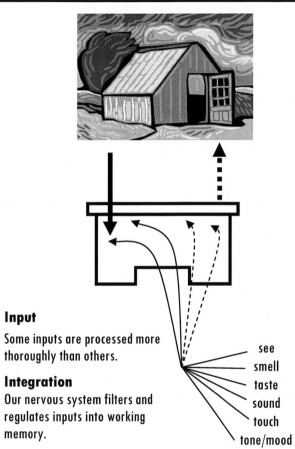

### Desktop Processing

Short-Term Working Memory Processing Level

### Sensory Input & Integration

Sensory Processing Level

**Elaboration**
How interconnected is the information?
How strong are the connections?

**Recall**
Where is the information stored?

**Process**
When we draw on what is in the barn in the processing phase, we enhance the likelihood that new information or skills will make their way into "the barn."

**Input**
Some inputs are processed more thoroughly than others.

**Integration**
Our nervous system filters and regulates inputs into working memory.

see
smell
taste
sound
touch
tone/mood

**Most inputs depart quickly.**

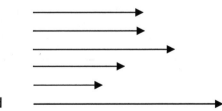

**WHAT WE KNOW ABOUT THE BRAIN & LEARNING**

Hearts pump. Lungs breathe. Brains learn. It's simple, functional biology. The human brain is born into existence needing to make sense of the world. It does this initially (first years) through redundancy and pattern seeking. From these early processes it evolves to make meaning ~ so that it can understand the stimuli entering it (many millions per second) and predict upcoming events ~ so as to be both safe (protected from harm) as well as to organize, plan, form perceptions of the world, apply experiences, interpret feelings, process for desired outcomes ~ in other words ~ LEARN.

As G. Christian Jernstedt of Dartmouth College states, "The biological limits to our potential are relatively minimal compared to the cultural and environmental limits. There are sound and weak techniques of learning and teaching, more than bright and dull minds. We can now consider our own philosophy of teaching, our own goals for what will happen for our students, the methods we use and would like to use to help our students learn, and the outcomes we typically achieve."

Given our new understandings, it is no longer sufficient to learn a body of knowledge or to perform a set of skills just to obtain a passing grade ~ and, ultimately, a degree to culminate our persistent efforts. In a vastly changing world, today's learner must do better than that. As instructors, we need to determine how to accommodate this shift on behalf of our learners ~ and with respect to their careers. Knowing for NOW is not acceptable. Knowing, understanding and applying OVER TIME must be the most rudimentary of outcomes (and clearly much beyond even that!). For tomorrow's needs, *ALL TEACHING (LEARNING) MUST BE DESIGNED FOR LONG-TERM MEMORY AND RECALL*. If we don't have it, or can't access it at appropriate times in the future... we've squandered opportunity and potential. Instructors work hard. We need to insist on a greater return on our investment.

If our motors are roaring and our tires are spinning... are we getting the traction needed for credible outcomes?

In his book on "Brain Based Teaching..." Robert Greenleaf (2005) provides a process, a framework for generating more efficiency and effectiveness. It is based on some straightforward thinking about the needs of instructors *and learners*. As the instructor, the following questions illustrate notions of what would make unit of study preparation and effort more targeted, and more effective in getting the results we desire.

1. How do I *invite* ALL learners to participate?

2. How can I organize the unit of study to *CAUSE* learners to do the thinking or processing of targeted course outcomes (for long-term memory)?

3. How can I help learners create multiple connections for sustained learning and recall? For application and transfer?

Dr. Patrick Levitt, neurobiologist at Vanderbilt University, states flat out, "Emotion *is* learning." He further states, "... human learning is identical to that of rats and monkeys" (in so far as their capacity takes them). "It is our process of growing (experiencing) which generates variations in experiences which affect cellular dispositions and predispositions." In other words, we come with some genetic hard wiring, however, we also have different and varied experiences as we grow which have an influence on our neural 'firings,' and the formation of more- or less-used pathways in our processing. These acculturated, cumulative activities influence connections made in our brain, and our ultimate disposition toward a given thing.

**APPENDIX D** | ## Instructional Best Practices

Although advances in neuroscience research have provided great insights into the human mind and what it takes to form memory, the field is relatively new, compared to the volumes of relevant literature from educational practices. Marzano, Pickering, and Pollock conducted a review of educational research over the past 35 years, condensing the most credible research into the salient practices that have the most impact on student achievement outcomes. The table below portrays the nine most effective, known practices. For a more detailed explanation of each, refer to the source as cited.

### "CLASSROOM INSTRUCTION THAT WORKS"
### Marzano, Pickering, Pollock ~ ASCD 2001

Categories of Instructional Strategies that Impact Student Achievement

| CATEGORY | PERCENTILE GAIN | NUMBER OF STUDIES |
|---|---|---|
| Identifying Similarities and Differences | 45% | 31 |
| Summarizing and Note Taking | 34% | 21 |
| Reinforcing Effort and Providing Recognition | 29% | 21 |
| Homework and Practice | 28% | 134 |
| Nonlinguistic Representation | 27% | 246 |
| Cooperative Learning | 27% | 122 |
| Setting Objectives and Providing Feedback | 23% | 63 |
| Generating and Testing Hypotheses | 23% | 63 |
| Questions, Cues, and Advance Organizers | 22% | 1,251 |

**APPENDIX E**

## The Natural Learning Systems

Understanding how the mind works to absorb inputs and process them to generate long-term memory and recall (not just rote use of terms and information), is fundamental to the design of approaches at the teaching or learning intersection. Dr. Barbara Given, of the Krasnow Institute at George Mason University, has developed a model of "5 Natural Learning Systems" that permeate brain functions and mind processing. Her work in understanding and translating this field of study into the educational and learning arenas has been conducted with great care and scrutiny for accuracy and usefulness. Each of the five systems spans across all lobes of the brain. Thus, it behooves us to be aware of, and to engage all systems in order to enhance memory and recall of important curriculum. The five natural learning systems are articulated in an abbreviated, bulleted format below. For a thorough rendition, please see Dr. Given's full work.

| | | Caveat |
|---|---|---|
| COGNITIVE LEARNING SYSTEM | ▪ Interprets, stores, and retrieves information via patterns and pictures<br>▪ Establishes integrated circuits of knowledge and skill | **Can be overrun by the stress response system and other perceived priorities** |
| EMOTIONAL LEARNING SYSTEM | ▪ Personal meaning ~ relevance ~ accelerates learning<br>▪ Empowers and energizes, or depresses and stifles, all other learning systems<br>▪ Manages a learner's motivation, demeanor, and creativity | **Operates internal stress response activities and generates memory enhancements or inhibitors** |
| SOCIAL LEARNING SYSTEM | ▪ Governs interactions and communications with others<br>▪ Teamwork and team accomplishments are integral to integrated systems<br>▪ Working together in pairs or in small groups to problem-solve, integrates systems | **Acquiring skills to work productively and effectively with all other types of people is essential** |
| PHYSICAL LEARNING SYSTEM | ▪ Gathers information through all senses<br>▪ Distributes information throughout the brain and the body<br>▪ Converts input into action ~ physical encoding and engagement promotes connection and ownership | **Takes longer to establish, however is sustained ~ like riding a bike** |
| REFLECTIVE LEARNING SYSTEM | ▪ Weighs past, present, and future projections<br>▪ Interprets verbal and nonverbal cues ~ monitoring mechanisms<br>▪ Meta-cognates: "Under this circumstance, in this environment, what do I need for understanding or performance?" | **Cognitive, Emotion, and Physical Systems always operate within a physical or perceptual context.** |

**APPENDIX F**

# Bi-Modal Memory Packets

## RESEARCH RESULTS FOR NONLINGUISTIC REPRESENTATION
and the Formation of Bi-Modal Memory Packets in Marzano et al. 2001

Categories of Instructional Strategies that Impact Student Achievement

RESEARCH
SYNOPSIS

**+27% impact on student performance outcomes**

- Variety of ways to accomplish the production of imagery in minds (NLRs)

  - Graphic representations created on paper or other medium.

  - Physical Models: Commonly thought of as manipulatives, or ways to engage learners in concrete representations of the idea, information, skill, pattern, or process.

  - Mental Pictures: Symbolic of the construct being learned; ways to help learners "feel" or consider circumstances regarding the topic or situation.

  - Drawing and Pictographs: Mind mapping, a la Buzan, or Clustering a la Rico ~ symbolic images or drawings that represent relationships, meanings, or importance ~ relative to other factors or information.

  - Kinesthetic: Using physical movement or positioning, to demonstrate, or replicate an idea, context, or flow of activity.

- Nonlinguistic Representations should elaborate knowledge, devising mental models to approximate concrete forms.

| AUTHOR OF THE STUDY | PERCENTILE GAIN IN STUDENT ACHIEVEMENT |
|---|---|
| Mayer, 1989 | 34% - 40% |
| Powell, 1980 | 34% |
| Hattie, 1996 | 32% |
| Walberg, 1999 | 34% - 21% |
| Fletcher, 1990 | 20% |
| Guzzetti, Snyder, & Glass, 1993 | 20% |

# APPENDIX G

## Assessment, Testing, & Data

**NEW PARADIGM FOR DIFFERENTIATED ASSESSMENT**

Assessment can play an important role in engaging students in their learning. Shifting student thinking away from what the instructor wants in order to achieve a grade ~ to a personal ownership of learning requires the development of new modes of performance assessment strategies. Assignments that connect student choice and higher-order thinking shift the emphasis of the class work from "doing," to "learning." When learners have the opportunity to select ways of showing evidence of their learning, the accountability for teaching and learning becomes a shared experience.

**PROJECT BASED ASSESSMENT**

**Step 1** The teacher clearly articulates the unit of study outcomes to be assessed, so that all students understand.

**Step 2** The teacher facilitates classroom discussion, developing essential questions that can be assessed. These must demonstrate the knowledge, skills, and attitudes needed to meet the unit of study outcome(s).

**Step 3** The teacher has students choose the essential question they plan to answer through the project design. This can be done individually, or in a collaborative, cooperative group. This is another opportunity for student choice.

Step **4**  The instructor discusses what feedback will be collected along the way *during* the project. Since assessment drives instruction," faculty have the opportunity to provide input into the project and/or teach/re-teach the needed skills to improve the quality of the learning outcomes.

Step **5**  The teacher and students interpret the results of the project, and connect the information to the essential question and learning outcomes.

Step **6**  Students engage in communicating the results of the project-based assessment to the critical audience.

Step **7**  Both the teacher and the students conduct an evaluation of the project, assessed through a rubric.

The following table is an elaborated version of that provided on pages 65-66. It intends to, in a general manner, illustrate approximate parallels of levels, quality of knowledge to be demonstrated, quantities of functions to be performed or demonstrated, and types of applications generated in context to curriculum, workplace, and/or world issues. Faculty assign point values to the assessment tasks and students choose what they will undertake in order to show evidence of their learning.

## Leveled Assignments & Student Choice

### Descriptions

**Level 1**

The instructor offers a wide variety of assignment choices to meet the individual learning styles of the students.

Assignments are developed to meet the outcomes of the unit of study. Students choose the tasks that have meaning to them.

These tasks represent a student's understanding of the basic knowledge of the unit of study and represent average competence, usually represented by a traditional C grade.

**Level 2**

This level represents tasks that require an application of skills acquired in level 1.

Students once again have the opportunity to choose the task or essential issues that have meaning to them. This level respects and appreciates student perspective and choice.

Assessment tasks usually require some research and extension from the class work in order to address the essential question.

Faculty coach disengaged learners to embrace these tasks, but these students tend to be very successful with such open ended activities.

**Level 3**

This level requires critical thinking and analysis of real-world challenges.

Innovative thinking about the application of knowledge outside the class work is expected.

Students engage with personnel in the field in order to gain a perspective on how classroom learning connects with the challenges in this global society.

Assessments are usually dense and require extended time to complete.

## Examples

**Level 1**

Develop a webpage.

Develop a book to teach the concept to another student.

Write a traditional report.

Write a book report.

Create a Power Point presentation.

Develop a computer program.

Develop a model, collage, or poster.

Develop a literature circle.

Design a board game.

Develop a brochure.

Build a class presentation and/or demonstration.

**Level 2**

Compare New England Patriots football (or other teams or sports) player statistics and show evidence of your work.

Summarize the most effective presidential ads and why.

Imagine you are in "this" dilemma. How would you react to the situation?

What exercises appear to have the greatest impact on cardio vascular fitness? Why?

Become aware of and/or involved in Community Service activities.

Read to elementary students.

Volunteer at the local senior citizen home or at the local hospital.

**Level 3**

Should all food additives be avoided?

What did the U.S. know about the attack on Pearl Harbor before it happened?

Who should win the next season's World Series?

In what way would your town be different if the Confederacy had won the war?

Will there be a cure for Alzheimer's disease in your lifetime? How do you know?

If John F Kennedy were alive today, what would his position be on the war in Iraq?

What are real-world community problems or challenges that need research based solutions?

## Traditional Grading & Differentiated Assessment Grid

| | Traditional Grading | Differentiated Assessments | | |
|---|---|---|---|---|
| | **Corresponding TRADITIONAL Grade** | **Evidence of KNOWLEDGE of Outcomes** | **Evidence of Knowledge and PERFORMANCE of Outcomes** | **Evidence of Knowledge, Performance, Critical Thinking, and APPLICATION of Outcomes** |
| Level 1 | C | 60 points | 10 points | |
| Level 2 | B | 10 points | 50 points | 10 points |
| Level 3 | A | | 10 points | 60 points |

# BIBLIOGRAPHY

## Administrator's Role

Guskey, Thomas. *"Does it make a Difference? Evaluating Professional Development,"* Educational Leadership, March 2002

Kirkpatrick, D. L. *Evaluating Training Programs.* American Society for Training and Development, Madison, Wisconsin, 1975.

"Killion, Joellen, *Results,* National Staff Development Council, January 2002.

Reeves, Douglas B. "The Learning Leader," ASCD 2006

www.nsdc.org

www.ascd.org

## Assessment, Testing, & Data

Black, Paul & Wiliam, Dylan. "Inside the Black Box: Raising Standards Through Classroom Assessment." *Phi Delta Kappan* Oct. 1998.

Black, Paul & Wiliam, Dylan. "Assessment and Classroom Learning." *Assessment in Education* Mar. 1998: p. 7-74.

Chappius, Jan. "Helping Students Understand Assessment." *Educational Leadership* Vol. 63 no. 3. Nov. 2005: p. 39.

Popham, James W. *The Truth About Testing: An Educator's Call to Action.* ASCD, 2001.

www.ascd.org

Reeves, Douglas. "Leading to Change: Closing the Implementation Gap," *Educational Leadership*, Vol. 64 no 6. Mar. 2007: p. 85.

http://www.mikeschmoker.com

Schmoker, Mike. *Results, The Key to Continuous School Improvement.* ASCD, 1996.

Shepard, Lorrie A. "Linking Formative Assessment to Scaffolding. *"Educational Leadership"* Vol. 63 no. 3. Nov. 2005: p. 66.

Stiggins, Rick. "Assessment Crisis: The Absence of Assessment FOR Learning." *Phi Delta Kappan* Vol. 83, No. 10. June 2002: p. 758-765.

www.pdkintl.org/kappan/k9911sti.htm

Stiggins, Rick. "Assessment, Student Confidence, and School Success." *Phi Delta Kappan* Aug. 2002.

Stiggins, Rick. "Assessment Through the Student's Eyes," Educating the Whole Child, *Educational Leadership*, Vol. 64 no 8. May 2007: p. 22.

White, Stephen H. *Beyond the Numbers: Making Data Work for Teachers & School Leaders.* Advanced Learning Press, 2005.

## Brain Sciences & Learning

Gerlic, I., and Jausovec, N. "Multimedia: Differences in Cognitive Processes Observed with EEG." *Educational Technology Research and Development.* 1999: 47 (3): 5-14.

Given, Barbara. *Teaching to the Brain's Natural Learning Systems.* ASCD, 2002.

bgiven@gmu.edu

Greenleaf, Robert K. *Brain Based Teaching: Making Connections for Long-Term Memory and Recall.* Greenleaf & Papanek Publications, P.O. Box 186, Newfield, Me. 04056, 2005.

www.greenleaflearning.com

Greenleaf, Robert K. & Wells-Papanek, Doris. *Memory, Recall, the Brain & Learning.* (Former Title: *Knowledge Representation and the Brain.*) Greenleaf & Papanek Publications, 2005.

www.greenleaflearning.com
www.tailoredlearningtools.com

Greenleaf, Robert K. "Motion and Emotion: Understanding the Essential Roles of Motion and Emotion in Brain Function..." *Principal Leadership,* NASSP. May 2003.

www.greenleaflearning.com

Jernstedt, G. Christian. *Perspectives on Learning, Teaching, and the Brain.* Dartmouth College, 2004.

Schenck, Jeb. *Learning, Teaching, and the Brain.* 2003. (self-published)

knowa@directairnet.com

Willis, Judy. *Research-Based Strategies to Ignite Student Learning.* ASCD, 2006.

jwillisneuro@aol.com
www.RADTeach.com

## Coaching Learning in the Classroom

Blackstein, Alan M. *Failure is NOT an Option*. Corwin Press, 2004.

Donegan, Billie, Greenleaf, Robert K., and Wells-Papanek, Doris. *Coaching Reluctant Learners*. Greenleaf & Papanek Publications, P.O. Box 186, Newfield, ME 04056, 2006.

Fried, Robert L. *The Game of School: Why We All Play It, How It Hurts Kids, and What It Will Take to Change It*. Jossey-Bass, 2005.

Fried, Robert L. *The Passionate Teacher: A Practical Guide (2nd Edition)*. Beacon Press, 2001.

McBride, William. *Entertaining an Elephant: A Novel About Learning and Letting Go*. University Editions, ©1996.

Howard, Gary R. "As Diversity Grows, So Must We," Responding to Changing Demographics, *Educational Leadership,* Vol. 64 no. 6. March 2007: p. 16.

Stewart, Vivien. "Becoming Citizens of the World," The Prepared Graduate, *Educational Leadership,* Vol. 64, no. 7. April 2007: p. 7.

Teaff, Grant. "Coaching in the Classroom: Teaching Self-Motivation," Cord Communications, 1994.

billiedonegan@yahoo.com
www.greenleaflearning.com
www.tailoredlearningtools.com

www.gse.harvard.edu

http://www.citrus.k12.fl.us/edserv/klaud
erm/Bill%20McBride.ppt

## Education: Instruction & Engagement

ASCD Associate News. *An "Insider's" View: What's Behind ASCD's Focus on Formative Assessment*. Winter Issue, 2007 p. 3.

Bottoms, Gene. *What Really Works?* Southern Regional Education Board, *High Schools That Work* Vol. 21. 2006.

gene.bottoms@sreb.org

Bottoms, Gene. *Closing the Achievement Gap*. Southern Regional Education Board, *High Schools That Work* Vol. 57. 2001.

www.sreb.org

Breneman, David W. et. al. *Remediation in Higher Education: A Symposium*. July, 1998. Report to Kansas State Board of Education.

Caine, Renate N., and Caine, Geoffrey. "The Way We Learn." *Educational Leadership* Vol. 64, no.1. Sept. 2006.

Deci, Edward, Ryan, Richard, and Koestner, Richard. "A Meta-Analytic Review of Experiments Examining the Effects of Extrinsic Rewards on Intrinsic Motivation." *Psychological Bulletin* Vol. 125. no.6. 1999.

Donegan, Billie, Greenleaf, Robert K., and Wells-Papanek, Doris. *Coaching Reluctant Learners*. Greenleaf & Papanek Publications, P.O. Box 186, Newfield, ME 04056, 2006.

billiedonegan@yahoo.com
www.greenleaflearning.com
www.tailoredlearningtools.com

DuFour, Richard & DuFour, Rebecca, Eaker, Robert, and Karhanek, Gayle. "*Whatever It Takes: How Professional Learning Communities Respond When Kids Don't Learn*," National Education Service, 2004.

E. D. Tab. *Adult Education Participation in 2004-05*. National Center for Education Statistics, May 2006.

Given, Barbara K. *Learning Styles: A Guide for Teachers and Parents*. Learning Forum Publications. Revised 2000.

bgiven@gmu.edu

Greenleaf, Robert K. *Brain Based Teaching: Making Connections for Long-term Memory and Recall*. Greenleaf & Papanek Publications, P.O. Box 186, Newfield, Me. 04056, 2005.

www.greenleaflearning.com

## Education: Instruction *&* Engagement cont.

Greenleaf, Robert K. *Creating and Changing Mindsets: Movies of the Mind.* Greenleaf & Papanek Publications, P.O. Box 186, Newfield, Me. 04056, 2005.

www.greenleaflearning.com

Greenleaf, Robert K. "Motion and Emotion: Understanding the Essential Roles of Motion and Emotion in Brain Function..." *Principal Leadership,* NASSP. May 2003.

www.greenleaflearning.com

Greenleaf, Robert K. & Wells-Papanek, Doris. *Memory, Recall, the Brain & Learning.* (Former Title: *Knowledge Representation and the Brain.*) Greenleaf & Papanek Publications, 2005.

www.greenleaflearning.com
www.tailoredlearningtools.com

Guskey, Thomas. "Mapping the Road to Proficiency." *Educational Leadership* Vol. 63. no. 3. Nov. 2005: p. 32.

http://www.schoolimprovement.com/presenters/thomas-guskey.html

Hunkings, Francis P. "Helping Students Ask Their Own Questions" *Social Education* Apr. 1985: p. 293-296.

Johnson & Johnson. Cooperative Learning.

www.co-operation.org/pages/cl-methods.html

Kagan. Cooperative Learning.

www.kaganonline.com

Kelly, Tom and Littleman, Jonathan. *The Art of Innovation,* Doubleday ~ Random House, Inc. 2001.

Kiewra, Kenneth A. "Memory-Compatible Instruction." Utah State University: *Engineering Education* Feb. 1987.

Kumar, David D. "A Meta-Analysis of the Relationship Between Science Instruction and Student Engagement," *Education Review* Vol. 43. Issue 1. 1991.

Lenehan, Miriam et. al. "Effects of Learning-Style Intervention On College Students' Achievement, Anxiety, Anger and Curiosity." Journal of College Student Development Vol. 35. no. 6. Nov. 1994: p. 461.

## Education: Instruction & Engagement cont.

Levine, Arthur. *Educating School Teachers*. The Education Schools Project, 2006.

Levine, Arthur. *A Higher Bar for Future Teachers*. Oct. 31, 2006.　　　www.boston.com/news/education/higher/articles

Marzano, Pickering, and Pollock. *Classroom Instruction That Works*. ASCD, 2001.

Pavio, Allan. *The Empirical Case for Dual Coding*, in: *Imagery, Memory, and Cognition: Essays in Honor of Allan Paivio*. (J. C. Yuille, ed.) *Lawrence Erlbaum Associates* Hillsdale, NJ: 1983.

Reeves, D. "Five Top Tips to Improve Student Engagement," Center for Performance Assessment, *CPA-00011680*, Dec. 2006.　　　http://www.makingstandardswork.com/aboutus/dr_douglas_reeves.htm

SCANS: Secretary's Commission on Achieving Necessary Skills, US Department of Labor, 200 Constitution Ave NW, Washington D.C. 20210.　　　http://wdr.doleta.gov/SCANS/whatwork/whatwork.pdf

Sadoski, M., Goetz, E.T., Olivarez, A., Jr., Lee, S. and Roberts, N.M. "*Imagination in Story Reading: The Role of Imagery, Verbal Recall, Story Analysis, and Processing Levels. Journal of Reading Behavior* Vol. 22. 1990: 55-70.

Willis, Judy. *Research-Based Strategies to Ignite Student Learning*. ASCD, 2006.

Willis, Judy. *Brain-Friendly Strategies for the Inclusion Classroom*. ASCD, 2007.　　　jwillisneuro@aol.com
www.RADTeach.com

Woloshyn, Vera, Wood, Eileen, Willoughby, Teena, and Pressley, Michael. *Elaborative Interrogation Facilitates Adult Learning of Factual Paragraphs. Journal of Educational Psychology* Vol. 82. no. 3. 1990.

## Student Choice

Brooks, Jacqueline G. and Brooks, Martin G. *The Case for Constructivist Classrooms*. Prentice Hall, 2001.

Donegan, Billie, Greenleaf, Robert K., and Wells-Papanek, Doris. *Coaching Reluctant Learners*. Greenleaf & Papanek Publications, P.O. Box 186, Newfield, ME 04056, 2006.

billiedonegan@yahoo.com
www.greenleaflearning.com
www.tailoredlearningtools.com

Greenleaf, Robert K. *Creating and Changing Mindsets: Movies of the Mind*. Greenleaf & Papanek Publications, P.O. Box 186, Newfield, Me. 04056, 2005.

www.greenleaflearning.com

Kohn, Alfie. "Unconditional Teaching." *Educational Leadership* Vol. 63. No.1. Sept. 2005: p. 20.

McCombs, Barbara and Whisler, Jo Sue. *The Learner-Centered Classroom and School*. John Wiley & Sons, Inc., 1997.

McCombs, Barbara. "Learner-Centered Principles and Technology." *TeacherLine* Jan. 2001.

Mitra, Dana L. "The Significance of Students: Can Increasing 'Student Voice' in Schools Lead to Gains in Youth Development?" *Teachers College Record* Vol. 106. Apr. 2004.

Reeves, D. "Five Top Tips to Improve Student Engagement," Center for Performance Assessment, CPA-00011680, Dec. 2006.

http://www.makingstandardswork.com/aboutus/dr_douglas_reeves.htm

## ABOUT THE AUTHORS

**Elaine M. Millen** has over twenty five years experience in education as a teacher, principal, director of special education, curriculum director and assistant superintendent of schools. She has taught at both the undergraduate and graduate level at both public and private institutions. She has worked with hundreds of school leaders across the country in areas related to curriculum, using data for decision making, and research based instructional practices. She is the co-developer of EMPHASIS, a standards implementation process for K-12 schools; and the Literacy for All System a middle and high school process for engaging content area teachers in defining a coherent literacy program. She was part of the Northeast Regional Laboratory at Brown University and was a consultant to the secondary reform project. elaine.millen@granite.edu

**Dr. Robert K. Greenleaf** Dr. Robert K. Greenleaf has taught at all grade levels, K-16, served as a professional development specialist at Brown University, and has 20 years of experience in public education, ranging from Superintendent of Schools to Assistant Superintendent of Schools, Elementary School Principal, Teacher, and Special Education Assistant. He is President of Greenleaf Learning, which specializes in educational strategies for understanding behaviors, building esteem and achievement, and brain-based learning for long-term memory and recall. Bob is the author of seven instructional books, as well as many articles. Bob holds a Doctorate in Education from Vanderbilt University, a Masters in Educational Administration, and a Bachelor's degree in Psychology. www.greenleaflearning.com

**Doris Wells-Papanek** is a design consultant and learning coach. She applies brain research to design tailored learning tools for education and business. In education, she works with students, teachers, faculty, administrators, and parents to empower learners to organize their time, tasks, and thoughts. In business, Doris works with designers, companies, and design schools to integrate users' mindsets and learning processes into sustainable product development. With over 25 years of experience in design, software, and education, Doris has co-authored five brain-based instructional books, developed corporate design strategies, managed user interface groups, taught design, researched and designed human-centered usability studies, and designed the appearance and behavior of software. www.tailoredlearningtools.com

**Sharyn L. Orvis** has over 20 years experience in urban and rural education PK-Grade 12. Certified as an English teacher, Reading Specialist and Principal, Sharyn has provided leadership in the school/district improvement process serving as Curriculum Coordinator, Director of Instructional Improvement, and Federal grants manager. She has worked to support teachers, paraprofessionals, students, their families, and communities. Sharyn has experience in professional development, curriculum revision, and data driven formative assessments for instruction. As the principal of a Title I School in Need of Improvement, she worked closely with staff and families to make a profound difference in school culture and student achievement, resulting in substantial *sustained* progress within two years. cntrywds@verizon.net

## *Greenleaf & Papanek* Publications  **BOOKS FOR SALE**

### COLLEGE EDITION

Stock ID: **ETS-C**  Price: **$27**

### GRADES 5-12 EDITION

Stock ID: **ETS-S**  Price: **$27**

### ENGAGING TODAY'S STUDENTS, What All Educators Need to Know *&* Be Able to Do

In these two editions of "Engaging Today's Students," we have examined the research around the learner of today, effective teaching practices, and the brain sciences that link to long-term memory and recall. We have observed hundreds of classroom lessons and activities, developed by an array of practicing educators. A strong indicator for how we organized this book was our deep commitment to learners ~ students as learners AND teachers as learners ~ and how we all can learn in significant and sustainable ways.

With a central focus on what today's learners require, we have created two editions, one with a focus on College level learners and the other referencing the needs of the grades 5-12 population of students. Each addresses the four essential learning components that drive student engagement.

### Memory, Recall, the Brain *&* Learning

Explore ways of incorporating brain-based instruction in the classroom. The power of combining verbal and visual representations into powerful bi-modal memory packets. Over 40 teacher and student generated activities, organizers, templates, and strategies. Improve student performance!

Stock ID: **MRBL**  Price: **$25**

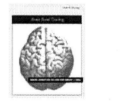

### Brain Based Teaching

Explore teaching and learning through three overarching lenses: How can I "frame" (design) the learning circumstance or activity to INVITE ALL learners, to participate? How can I design the learning experience to CAUSE learner processing ~ the work required for sustained learning and recall? How do I engineer tasks that create opportunities for multiple PATHWAYS (connections) to be formed for integration, application, & recall?

Stock ID: **BBT**  Price: **$24**

### Coaching Reluctant Learners

This book provides today's middle and high school teachers with the tools they need to ensure classroom success for today's students in a practical framework ~ unit-by-unit, where both teacher and student can feel more successful. Embedded in this book are proven strategies, activities, examples, and a framework for units that will improve student motivation and performance.

Stock ID: **CRL**  Price: **$27**

### A Mastery Toolkit

Speaking directly to the student, this book explores the foundations of understanding, essential strategies, and learning tools to become motivated, independently engaged in the learning process, responsible for learning, and accountable for making good choices. The goal is to become a "Can Do" Student ~ a student who takes charge of their learning and empowers themselves in ways to be successful.

Stock ID: **AMT**  Price: **$25**

### Creating *&* Changing Mindsets

If rational behavior was the basis for human interaction and the mysteries of learning and development were well understood ~ this book wouldn't be needed. Clear strategies to assist "shifts" in attitude and behavior are included. The question, "will this change last?" plagues us every year. Here's how to impact changes within a month's time... for long-term, sustained differences!

Stock ID: **CCM**  Price: **$24**

*Greenleaf & Papanek* **Publications**

PO Box 186 Newfield, Maine 04056

## BOOK ORDER FORM

Please mail this form, to the above address, with a check, or

Fax a Purchase Order to:          fax 847.615.9958

bob@greenleaflearning.com       tel 207.793.8675
doris@tailoredlearningtools.com  tel 847.615.9957

NAME

CO/ORG/SCHOOL

ADDRESS

CITY

STATE/ZIP CODE

EMAIL

TELEPHONE

CHECK or PO #

DATE

Make checks payable to **GREENLEAF LEARNING**.

| STOCK ID | QUANTITY | PRICE | TOTALS | STEPS | DISCOUNT CALCULATOR |
|---|---|---|---|---|---|
| ETS-C college | | x $27 | = | **1** Enter the "Quantity" of each book you are buying | |
| ETS-S grades 5-12 | | x $27 | = | | 2 books total = $1 discount per book |
| MRBL | | x $25 | = | **2** Add the total number of books and multiply by the "discount" amount using the "Discount Calculator" | 3 books total = $2 discount per book |
| BBT | | x $24 | = | | 4 books total = $3 discount per book |
| CRL | | x $27 | = | | 5-10 books total = $4 discount per book |
| AMT | | x $25 | = | **3** Multiply "Quantity" x "Price" and enter the amounts due for each book in the "Totals" column | |
| CCM | | x $24 | = | | |
| discount | x       = | subtotal | = | **4** Add the extended total in the "Subtotal" box | **For Discounts on Bulk Orders Over 10 Books Total: Call 207.793.8675** |
| | | less discount | - | **5** Subtract the quantity discount and then add shipping fees to arrive to your final "TOTAL COST." | |
| | | total | = | | |
| | | shipping 1-4 books | + $3.50 | | |
| additional shipping for more than 4 books add .50 cents each | | | + | For more information, please visit our websites: www.greenleaflearning.com www.tailoredlearningtools.com | |
| | | Canada add $3.00 | + | | |
| | | **TOTAL COST** | = | | |